THREE PHILOSOPHIES OF LIFE

PETER KREEFT

Three Philosophies of Life

Ecclesiastes: Life as Vanity
Job: Life as Suffering
Song of Songs: Life as Love

IGNATIUS PRESS   SAN FRANCISCO

for John Mallon

who *knows*

Cover by Riz Boncan Marsella

ISBN 978-0-89870-262-0 (PB)
ISBN 978-1-68149-591-0 (eBook)
Library of Congress catalogue number 89-84054
Printed in the United States of America

CONTENTS

INTRODUCTION

The Inexhaustibility of Wisdom Literature

I have been a philosopher for all of my adult life, and the three most profound books of philosophy that I have ever read are Ecclesiastes, Job, and Song of Songs. In fact, the book that first made me a philosopher, at about age fifteen, was Ecclesiastes.

Books of philosophy can be classified in many ways: ancient versus modern, Eastern versus Western, optimistic versus pessimistic, theistic versus atheistic, rationalistic versus irrationalistic, monistic versus pluralistic, and many others. But the most important distinction of all, says Gabriel Marcel, is between "the full" and "the empty", the solid and the shallow, the profound and the trivial. When you have read all the books in all the libraries of the world, when you have accompanied all the world's sages on all their journeys into wisdom, you will not have found three more profound books than Ecclesiastes, Job, and Song of Songs.

These three books are literally inexhaustible. They brim with a mysterious power of renewal. I continually find new nourishment in rereading them, and I never tire of teaching them. They quintessentially exemplify my definition of a classic. A classic is like a cow: it gives fresh milk every morning. A classic is a book that rewards endlessly repeated rereading. A classic is like the morning, like nature herself: ever young, ever renewing. No, not even like nature, for she, like us, is doomed to die. Only God is ever young, and only the Book he inspired never grows old.

When God wanted to inspire some philosophy, why would he inspire anything but the best? But the best is not necessarily the most sophisticated. Plato says, in the *Ion*, that the gods deliberately chose the poorest poets to inspire the greatest poems so that the glory would be theirs, not man's. It is exactly what Saint Paul says in 1 Corinthians. And we see this principle at work throughout the Bible: the striking contrast between the primitiveness of the poet and the profundity of the poem, between the smallness of the singer and the greatness of the song, between the absence of human sophistication and the presence of divine *sophia*, divine wisdom. Something is always *breaking through* the words, something you can never fully grasp but also never fully miss if only you stand there with uncovered soul. Stand in the divine rain, and seeds of wisdom will grow in your soul.

Three Philosophies of Life

There are ultimately only three philosophies of life, and each one is represented by one of the following books of the Bible:

1. Life as vanity: Ecclesiastes
2. Life as suffering: Job
3. Life as love: Song of Songs

No more perfect or profound book has ever been written for any one of these three philosophies of life. Ecclesiastes is the all-time classic of vanity. Job is the all-time classic of suffering. And Song of Songs is the all-time classic of love.

The reason these are the only three possible philosophies of life is because they represent the only three places or conditions in which we can be. Ecclesiastes' "vanity" represents Hell. Job's suffering represents Purgatory.[1] And Song of Songs' love represents Heaven. All three conditions begin here and now on earth. As C. S. Lewis put it, "All that seems earth is Hell or Heaven." It is a shattering line, and Lewis added this one to it: "Lord, open not too often my weak eyes to this."

---

[1] Note to Protestant readers: please do not throw this book away just yet. I am not presupposing or trying to convert anyone to the Catholic doctrine of Purgatory. Here I mean by *Purgatory* any suffering that purges the soul. It begins in this life. If it is completed in the next, you can just as well call it Heaven's bathroom, if you like. A sanctification by any other name would smell as sweet.

The essence of Hell is not suffering but vanity, not pain but purposelessness, not physical suffering but spiritual suffering. Dante was right to have the sign over Hell's gate read: "Abandon all hope, ye who enter here."

Suffering is not the essence of Hell, because suffering can be hopeful. It was for Job. Job never lost his faith and his hope (which is faith directed at the future), and his suffering proved to be purifying, purgative, educational: it gave him eyes to see God. That is why we are all on earth.

Finally, Heaven *is* love, for Heaven is essentially the presence of God, and God is essentially love. ("God *is* love.")

Three Metaphysical Moods

Heidegger begins one of his most haunting books with the most haunting question: *"Why is there anything rather than nothing?"* He speaks of three moods that raise this great question. They are three metaphysical moods, three moods that reveal not just the feelings of the individual but also the meanings of being. And these three are the three metaphysical moods that give rise to the three philosophies of life that we find in Ecclesiastes, Job, and Song of Songs. Heidegger says,

"Why is there anything rather than nothing?". . .

Many men never encounter this question, if by encounter we mean not merely to hear and read about it as an interrogative formulation but to ask the question, that is, to bring it about, to raise it, to feel its inevitability.

And yet each of us is grazed at least once, perhaps more than once, by the hidden power of this question, even if he is not aware of what is happening to him. The question looms in moments of great despair, when things tend to lose all their weight and all meaning becomes obscured. Perhaps it will strike but once like a muffled bell that rings into our life and gradually dies away. It is present in moments of rejoicing, when all the things around us are transfigured and seem to be there for the first time, as if it might be easier to think they are not than to understand that they are and are as they are. The question is upon us in boredom, when we are equally removed from despair and joy, and everything about us seems so hopelessly commonplace that we no longer care whether anything is or is not—and with this the question "Why is there anything rather than nothing?" is evoked in a particular form.

But this question may be asked expressly, or, unrecognized as a question, it may merely pass through our lives like a brief gust of wind.

Despair is Job's mood. His suffering is not only bodily but also spiritual. What has he to look forward to except death? He has lost everything, even God—especially God, it seems.

Joy is the mood of love, young love, new love, "falling in love". That is the wonder in Song of Songs: that the beloved should *be*; that life should *be*; that anything, now all lit by the new light of love, should *be*—as mysterious a glory as it was to Job a mysterious burden.

Boredom is the mood of Ecclesiastes. It is a modern mood. Indeed, there is no word for it in any ancient language! In this mood, there is neither a reason to die, as in Job, nor a reason to live, as in Song of Songs. This is the deepest pit of all.

Three Theological Virtues

These three books also teach the three greatest things in the world, the three "theological virtues": faith, hope, and charity.

The lesson Ecclesiastes teaches is faith, the necessity of faith, by showing the utter vanity, the emptiness, of life without faith. Ecclesiastes uses only reason, human experience, and sense observation of life "under the sun" as instruments to see and think with; he does not add the eye of faith; and this is not enough to save him from the inevitable conclusion of "vanity of vanities". Then the postscript to the book, in the last few verses, speaks the word of faith. This is not proved by reason or sense observation, as in the rest of the book. This word of faith is the only one big enough to fill the silence of vanity. The word that answers Ecclesiastes' quest and gives the true answer to the question of the meaning of life is known only by faith: "Fear God and keep his commandments, for this is the whole duty of man. For God will bring every deed into judgment, with every secret thing, whether good or evil." Ecclesiastes has intellectual faith; he believes God exists. But that is not enough. "The demons also believe, and tremble" (James 2:19). Ecclesiastes proves the need for real faith, true faith, lived faith, saving faith, by showing the consequences of its absence, even in the presence of intellectual faith.

Job's lesson is hope. Job has nothing else but hope. Everything else is taken away from him. But hope alone enables him to endure and to triumph.

Song of Songs is wholly about love, the ultimate meaning of life, the greatest thing in the world.

These three books also give us an essential summary of the spiritual history of the world. G. K. Chesterton did that in three sentences: "Paganism was the biggest thing in the world, and Christianity was bigger, and everything since has been comparatively small." Job shows us the heights of pre-Christian hope and heroism. It is not strictly pagan, of course, but it is not yet Christian. Song of Songs shows us the spiritual center of the Christian era, the era the modern secular establishment has told such incredible lies about, the Middle Ages. Finally, Ecclesiastes tells us the truth about the modern, post-Christian world and world view: once the divine Lover's marriage offer is spurned, the modern divorcée cannot simply return to being a pagan virgin, any more than an individual who spurns Heaven and chooses Hell can make Hell into Purgatory, hopelessness into hope.

"The Divine Comedy" before Dante

In these three books of the Bible we have Dante's great epic *The Divine Comedy* played out, from Hell to Purgatory to

Heaven. But it is played out in our hearts and lives, not externalized into cosmic places, circles, stairs, and airs. And it is played out here and now, as seeds, though it is completed after death, as flowers.

There is movement between these three books, just as there is in *The Divine Comedy*. First, there is movement from Ecclesiastes to Job, like Dante's movement from Hell to Purgatory. This is found in the last two verses of Ecclesiastes. The conclusion of the rest of Ecclesiastes is "vanity", but the conclusion of the last two verses is: "Fear God and keep his commandments, for this is the whole duty of man. For God will bring every work into judgment, with every secret thing, whether good or evil." This is precisely the philosophy Job lives, and the result is that Job finds God and moves through Purgatory to Heaven.

And this is the second movement: from Job to Song of Songs. It takes place at the end of Job, when Job finally sees God's face. Ecclesiastes is the sunset, the end of hope; Job is the night with hope of morning; Song of Songs is the morning, which already begins to dawn at the end of Job. Song of Songs begins when God appears to Job, for where God is, there is love.

Love is the final answer to Ecclesiastes' quest, the alternative to vanity, and the meaning of life. But we cannot appreciate it until we look deeply at the question. This question is more than a question; it is a quest, a lived question. Scripture invites us on this quest, this journey through the night to the Rising Son. It is life's greatest journey. Will you climb aboard the great old ark of the Bible with me? I will try to call out to you what I see as we take this journey together. For that is really all a teacher can do.

ECCLESIASTES:
Life as Vanity

The Greatness of Ecclesiastes

The Bible is the greatest of books, and Ecclesiastes is the only book of philosophy, pure philosophy, mere philosophy, in the Bible. It is no surprise, then, that Ecclesiastes is the greatest of all books of philosophy.

What? Ecclesiastes the greatest of all books of philosophy? But the author does not even know the dialogues of Plato, or the logic of Aristotle, or even the rules of good outlining! He rambles, frequently changes his mind, and lets his moods move him almost as much as his evidence. How can this sloppy old tub be the Noah's ark of philosophy books? Furthermore, the whole point of this book is "vanity of vanities", the meaninglessness of human life. How could a book about meaninglessness be so meaningful?

The first objection could be answered by realizing that greatness comes not from the form but from the content. The form of Ecclesiastes is simple, direct, and artless. But the content, as we shall see, is the greatest thing that philosophy can ever say.

But what of the second objection? How can a book about meaninglessness be meaningful? A great book must be sincere, must practice what it preaches. For instance, the *Tao Te Ching*, that great Chinese classic (*ching*) about the spiritual power (*te*) of the Way (*Tao*), itself wields a mysterious spiritual power (*te*) over the reader, a power of the same subtle, waterlike, irresistible nature as the Tao itself. Or a great book about violence and passion, like a Dostoyevski novel, must itself be violent and passionate. A book about piety must be pious. And thus a book about vanity must be vain, must it not?

No. The philosopher who wrote Ecclesiastes is the *least* vain of philosophers. Vanity cannot detect itself, just as folly cannot detect itself. Only the wise know folly; fools know neither wisdom nor folly. Just as it takes wisdom to know folly, light to know darkness, it takes profundity to know vanity, meaning to know meaninglessness. Pascal says, "Anyone who does not see the vanity of life must be very vain indeed."

15

Compared with the neat little nostrums of comfort-mongering minds who cross our *t*'s and dot our *i*'s, Ecclesiastes is as great, as deep, and as terrifying as the ocean. If this philosopher were alive today and knew the reigning philosophy in America, pop psychology, with its positive strokings, OKs, narcissistic self-befriendings, panderings, patronizings, and bland assurances of "Peace! Peace!" when there is no peace, I think he would quote John Stuart Mill that it is better to be Socrates dissatisfied than a pig satisfied; and William Barrett: "It is better to encounter one's own existence in despair than never to encounter it at all."

Ecclesiastes has been called the greatest book ever written by passionate pessimists and God-haunted agnostics like Herman Melville, who says, in chapter 97 of *Moby Dick*, that "the truest of all books is *Ecclesiastes*". And Thomas Wolfe says, in chapter 47 of his classic American novel *You Can't Go Home Again*,

> Of all that I have ever seen or learned, that book seems to me the noblest, the wisest, and the most powerful expression of man's life upon this earth, and also the highest flower of poetry, eloquence and truth. I am not given to dogmatic judgments in the matter of literary creation, but if I had to make one, I could only say that *Ecclesiastes* is the greatest single piece of writing I have ever known, and the wisdom expressed in it the most lasting and profound.

If we find nothing in our first reading of Ecclesiastes to confirm this judgment, we had better read again. For we must either cavalierly dismiss the verdict of giants or climb onto their shoulders and look again. Does it not seem at least likely that it is the dwarf rather than the giant who misreads the landscape?

I have a friend who camps in the Maine woods each summer. One day he met an old hermit who had not lived in "civilization" for forty years. He seemed uncannily wise (at least wiser than secular people in our civilization, though not wiser than a

Christian), and when my friend asked him where he got his wisdom, he pulled from his pocket the only book he had had for forty years. It was a tattered, yellow copy of Ecclesiastes. Only Ecclesiastes. That one book had been enough for him. Perhaps "civilization" is so unwise because nothing is ever enough for it. The old hermit had stayed in one place, physically, and spiritually, and explored its depths; civilization, meanwhile, had moved restlessly on, skimming over the surface of the great deeps. While civilization was reading the *Times*, he was reading the eternities.

Ecclesiastes as Ethics

Ecclesiastes would be classified by premodern philosophers as a book about ethics, because it poses the most important of all ethical questions, the question all the great ethical classics are most fundamentally about: Plato's *Republic*, Aristotle's *Nicomachean Ethics*, Augustine's *Confessions*, Aquinas' "Treatise on Happiness" in the *Summa*, Pascal's *Pensées*, Spinoza's *Ethics*, Kierkegaard's *Either/Or*: the question of the summum bonum, the greatest good, highest value, ultimate end, or meaning of life.

Ancient ethics always dealt with three questions. Modern ethics usually deals with only one, or at the most two. The three questions are like the three things a fleet of ships is told by its sailing orders. (The metaphor is from C. S. Lewis.) First, the ships must know how to avoid bumping into each other. This is social ethics, and modern as well as ancient ethicists deal with it. Second, they must know how to stay shipshape and avoid sinking. This is individual ethics, virtues and vices, character building, and we hear very little about this from our modern ethical philosophers. Third, and most important of all, they must know why the fleet is at sea in the first place. What is their mission, their destination? This is the question of the summum bonum, and no modern philosophers except the existentialists seem even to be interested in this, the greatest of all questions. Perhaps that is why most modern philosophy seems so weak and wimpy, so specialized and elitist, and above all so boring, to ordinary people.

I think I know why modern philosophers dare not raise this greatest of questions: because they have no answer to it. It is a hole so big that only the courage of an existentialist or the faith of a theist can fill it.

Ecclesiastes the Existentialist

The first existentialist was not Sartre, though he coined the term. Nor was it Kierkegaard or Nietzsche, though most of the textbooks say so. Nor was it even Pascal, though he foreshadowed half of Kierkegaard and was the first to write about the fundamental existential experience of cosmic anxiety and meaninglessness. It was not even Saint Augustine, whose *Confessions* stands out as the profoundest example of depth psychology and existential autobiography ever written. It was not even Socrates, who alone among the philosophers totally existed his philosophy.

Rather, the first existentialist was Solomon, or whoever wrote Ecclesiastes. Here, some twenty-five hundred years before Sartre's *Nausea*, Camus' *The Stranger*, Beckett's *Waiting for Godot*, or Kafka's *The Castle*, we have the fundamental experience and intuition of each of these modern classics, expressed more candidly, directly, and artlessly than ever before or ever again.

If you are familiar with existentialist writings such as the four just mentioned, you will see the truth of this claim as we lift the curtain on Ecclesiastes. There is no need to stretch Ecclesiastes to fit the existentialist clothing.

The Modernity of Ecclesiastes

There is a book called *A Time to Live and a Time to Die*, by Robert Short, author of *The Gospel According to Peanuts*. It is a book of photographs, one for each verse of Ecclesiastes. The photographs are all contemporary. They are photos of things we see every day without noticing them. (Photography helps us to do just that: to notice instead of just to see.) These photographs are startlingly apt. They show the utter contemporaneity, the utter modernity, of Ecclesiastes, the perennially up-to-date book.

It is fitting that Ecclesiastes, of all books, should be illustrated by photographs, because Ecclesiastes is a series of word photographs. The word *photograph* literally means "light writing", a picture taken with light, "under the sun". That is the method of Ecclesiastes: simple observation. Unlike all the other books in the Bible, it has no faith flashbulb attached to its camera to reveal the inner depths or hidden meanings of life. It uses only the available light "under the sun": sense observation and human reason. The surface of life appears in this book with total clarity, brutal honesty, and spiritual poverty. Ecclesiastes is the truest picture of the surface that has ever been written.

Whatever rabbis first decided to include Ecclesiastes in the canon of sacred Scripture were both wise and courageous— wise because we appreciate a thing only by contrast, and Ecclesiastes is the contrast, the alternative, to the rest of the Bible, the question to which the rest of the Bible is the answer. There is nothing more meaningless than an answer without its question. That is why we need Ecclesiastes.

The rabbis were also courageous, because the question Ecclesiastes raises is so deep that only an answer that is deeper still can satisfy the mind and heart that dare to ask it, and if such an answer is not forthcoming, we must either run from the question in a dishonest cover-up or run from life in despair. These are the two running sores that plague the modern world.

Ecclesiastes is the one book in the Bible that modern man needs most to read, for it is Lesson One, and the rest of the Bible is Lesson Two, and modernity does not heed Lesson Two because it does not heed Lesson One. Whenever I teach the Bible as a whole, I always begin with Ecclesiastes. In another age, we could begin with God's beginning, Genesis. But in this age, the Age of Man, we must begin where our patient is; we must begin with Ecclesiastes.

Ecclesiastes is modern in at least seven ways.

First, it is an existential book, a book about human existence. It asks the great question of modern man: Does my existence here have any meaning at all? Previous ages disputed about *what* the meaning of human existence was. Ecclesiastes, alone among premodern books, dares to ask the question: Suppose it has none at all? Its question is not the essence but the existence of the meaning of life.

Second, it shows modernity's greatest fear, which is not so much the fear of death (that was ancient man's deepest fear), or the fear of sin or guilt or Hell (that was medieval man's deepest fear), but the fear of meaninglessness, of "vanity", of "the existential vacuum", the fear of Nothingness.

Third, it shares the best feature of the modern mind as well as the worst. Although it is a deeply despairing book, it is also a deeply honest book. Despair itself can be hopeful if it is honest. (We see a striking case of this in Job.)

Fourth, its answer to the question of the summum bonum, the greatest good, final end, or meaning of life, is the modern answer, namely, no answer. Of the twenty-one great civilizations that have existed on our planet, according to Toynbee's reckoning, ours, the modern West, is the first that does not have or teach its citizens any answer to the question why they exist. A euphemistic way of saying this is that our society is pluralistic and leaves us free to choose or create our own ultimate values. A more candid way of saying the same thing is that our society has nothing but its own ignorance to give us on this, the most important of all questions. As society grows, it knows more and more about less and less. It knows more about the little things and less about the big things. It knows more about every thing and less about Everything. Fifth, the practical result of this vacuum in values is hedonism. When you do not know why you do anything else, you can still "grab the gusto", "seize the day". When ultimate ends disappear, toys remain. Ecclesiastes' only positive advice is to follow Freud's "pleasure principle" but to be honest enough to remember that "this too is vanity" and that it ends only in death, that you cannot take any of your toys with you. There are flowers, but there is always a grinning skull behind the flowers. There are many pleasant recreations on the deck of the *Titanic*.

Even so, to "stop and smell the roses" is better advice than to pretend that our little hectic diversions are ultimately meaningful and satisfying. Honest hedonism is spiritually superior to dishonest self-delusion. Jesus had harsher words for the man who built greater barns to store his grain and said to his soul, "Soul, take your ease", than for the convicted prostitute or the thief on the cross. Infinitely superior to self-satisfied yuppiedom, Ecclesiastes has the heroism of honesty. Infinitely superior to pop psychology, it rises to the dignity of despair.

Sixth, its context, the world in which it carries on its research, is a secularized world. In that world, religion is reduced to one of many small departments of life, between "Press" and "Science" in the index of *Time* magazine. It is then further reduced to what can be empirically observed of this department of life.

In a secular world, religion is somewhere in life, not vice versa. God is an ingredient in my life rather than I an ingredient in his. Secularism is anthropocentric, not theocentric. The sacred may be allowed to exist, but it is defined by the secular rather than the secular being defined by the sacred, as in the rest of the Bible and in the rest of the premodern world.

A seventh way in which Ecclesiastes is modern is the most important one of all. Not only its observational context but also its method, its epistemology, its answer to the question: How do you know the truth? is wholly secular. The author is a reporter for earth's universal newspaper. He has not been privy to any special divine revelation or supernatural intervention. His God is simply "nature and nature's God", the God of our modern establishmentarian religion. He is an empiricist.

God's Silence in Ecclesiastes

The difference between philosophy and religion is the difference between speaking and listening, between man's speaking about God and God's speaking about man with man listening. This is the difference between reason and faith. Philosophy is man's search for God; the Bible is the story of God's search for man. Philosophy is words flying up; the Bible is the Word sent down. Ecclesiastes is the only book in the Bible in which God is totally silent. The author appeals to no divine revelation, only to natural human reason and sense observation. God is only the *object* of his quest, not the subject; the questee, not the quester, the Hound of Heaven.

In Job, God is also silent, except for the beginning and the ending. But these two passages make the difference between Job and Ecclesiastes. Because God speaks, Job has everything even though he has nothing. Because God is silent, Ecclesiastes has nothing even though he has everything.

God speaks twice in Job. In the first two chapters, we see him questioning Job, testing Job. In light of this beginning, we the readers understand the long middle section, Job's quest for God, as really God's quest for Job. But Job did not have those first two chapters. God seems silent to him, just as he did to Ecclesiastes.

In the last five chapters of Job, God speaks out of the storm. Nothing in all the world's literature is more profound than this speech. It is enough to satisfy Job, the hardest man on earth to satisfy. For Job is not patient. Job is impatient. Job is from Missouri: "Show me." Whatever is hidden in these chapters is great enough to satisfy the hardest man in the world to satisfy concerning the hardest question in the world, the mystery of evil. It would also be great enough to satisfy Ecclesiastes if God had spoken it to him, but he did not.

Perhaps Ecclesiastes just was not listening. In Job God showed up only when Job shut up. Job's best words are: "The words of Job are ended." As Elihu says to Job, "God is speaking all the time, first in one way, then in another, but we don't hear." Or perhaps Job got his answer and Ecclesiastes did not because Job was a suffering servant while Ecclesiastes was a mere philosopher. Ecclesiastes was like Socrates; Job was like Christ.

All of the Bible is divine revelation, divine speech. But God never speaks directly in Ecclesiastes. Ecclesiastes is all monologue, not dialogue. How is it divine revelation?

It is inspired monologue. God in his providence has arranged for this one book of mere rational philosophy to be included in the canon of Scripture because this too is divine revelation. It is divine revelation precisely in being the absence of divine revelation. It is like the silhouette of the rest of the Bible. It is what Fulton Sheen calls "black grace" instead of "white grace", revelation by darkness rather than by light. In this book God reveals to us exactly what life is when God does not reveal to us what life is. Ecclesiastes frames the Bible as death frames life.

The Summary of Ecclesiastes

The structure of Ecclesiastes is much more tight, much more logical, than it seems at first sight. The book seems to ramble, to go nowhere, to have no tightly argued deductions, only bits of wisdom sprinkled over a desert landscape like a few raindrops, quickly absorbed by the dry soil, or like a collage of photos taken through the porthole of a sinking ship.

Yet the book's rambling is deliberate, for this form perfectly expresses its content, its message: that *life* rambles to nowhere. Ecclesiastes practices what it preaches. Its form is one with its content: the test of great poetry. Does life chase its own tail? Very well, this book will do the same. Its ending and its beginning are identical: "All is vanity."

Ecclesiastes is, nevertheless, a logical argument, not just scattered observations. And its argument is deductive and demonstrative, not just inductive and observational. Though the author has never read Aristotle or any logic textbook and did not consciously intend his book to take the form of a syllogism, nevertheless it *is* a syllogism, simply because that is the form in which the human mind naturally and instinctively argues. My summary of Ecclesiastes in a syllogism (see page 35) is not a palimpsest but an X-ray; it does not impose a new or alien piture but reveals the structure already there, the bones beneath the flesh.

The argument of Ecclesiastes is summarized in the first three verses, amplified for twelve chapters, and then summarized at the end. The first three verses are the whole book in miniature. The first verse gives the title and author; the second verse gives the point, the conclusion; and the third verse gives the essential argument for it.

1. The words of the Preacher, son of David, king in Jerusalem.
2. Vanity of vanities, says the Preacher, Vanity of vanities! All is vanity.
3. What does man gain by all the toil at which he toils under the sun?

The Author of Ecclesiastes

The title of the original book is its first words. (Thus ancient authors outwit modern editors and publishers who obsessively change titles.) The title is not Ecclesiastes, "The Preacher", but

"The *Words* of the Preacher". It is not an autobiography but a sermon. Who "the Preacher" really was does not even matter. What matters is not the singer but the song. Like Buddha, the Preacher says, "Look not to me, look to my *dharma* [my doctrine]."
So we need not take sides in the scholarly controversy about authorship. The minority view, taken by conservative scholars, claims that the author was literally King Solomon, "the son of David, king in Jerusalem". The majority view claims that the style and vocabulary of the book strongly indicate another author. ("Strongly indicate", not "prove"; textual scholarship, like medicine, is not an exact science, though many of its practitioners act as if it were.) The majority view is that the book was written centuries after Solomon, during or after the Babylonian exile.

Even if this latter view is true, there is, of course, no plagiarism or attempt to deceive. It was a literary device of ancient Jewish authors to call themselves "Solomon", thus (1) humbly preserving their own anonymity and (2) declaring their indebtedness to their teacher and model, the ideal wise man. Where modern authors parade themselves and their newness even when they are small and their books are warmed-over unoriginalities, ancient authors had the opposite fashion: to make themselves small even when they were great and to declare their books traditional even when they were innovative. Fashions change; what remains is the need to be wary of all fashionable labels.

Since we need to call the author something, let us use the name "Solomon"—an appropriate name, whether literal or symbolic.

Solomon's point, or conclusion, is so blatant that only the sleeping could miss it. It is stated five times in the first verse (Eccl 1:2), exemplified for twelve chapters, and then repeated three times more in the last verse (Eccl 12:8), like the simple-minded preacher's "three-point sermon technique": "First I tells 'em what I'm gonna say. Then I says it. Then I tells 'em what I said." If you miss these three trumpets of doom, you are worse than asleep; you are dead.

The point is "vanity". What does "vanity" mean? Not, of course, the "vanity" of a "vanity mirror", which is narcissism, but "in vain", "useless", "profitless". The Hebrew word means literally "a chasing after wind", a grasping after shadows, a wild-goose chase. And there is no wild goose. There is no end (*telos*, purpose), only an end (*finis*, finish), namely, death. What we need more than anything else in the world, a reason to live and a reason to die—this simply does not exist.

Archibald MacLeish dramatizes this haunting horror in his poem "The End of the World". The image of life as a silly circus frames the picture:

> Quite unexpectedly as Vasserot
> The armless ambidextrian was lighting
> A match between his great and second toe
> And Ralph the Lion was engaged in biting
> The neck of Madame Sossman while the drum
> Pointed, and Teeny was about to cough
> In waltz-time swinging Jocko by the thumb—
> Quite unexpectedly the top blew off.
>
> And there, there overhead, there, there, hung over
> Those thousands of white faces, those dazed eyes,
> There in the starless dark, the poise, the hover,
> There with vast wings across the canceled skies,
> There in the sudden blackness, the black pall
> Of nothing, nothing, nothing—nothing at all.

Another terrifying portrait of Nothingness in the place of God is Ernest Hemingway's classic little short story "A Clean, Well-Lighted Place":

> It was not fear or dread. It was a Nothing that he knew too well. It was all a Nothing and a man was Nothing too. It was only that and light was all it needed and a certain cleanliness and order. Some lived in it and never felt it but he knew it all was nada y

pues nada y nada y pues nada. Our nada, who are in nada, nada be thy name thy kingdom nada thy will be nada in nada as it is nada. Give us this nada our daily nada and nada us our nada as we nada our nadas and nada us not into nada but deliver us from nada; pues nada. Hail nothing, full of nothing, nothing is with thee . . .

Nada, Spanish for "nothing", is the word Saint John of the Cross, greatest of mystics, used to describe God, the sheer abyss of pure Being, beyond all finite beings, beyond some-things. He called God *todo y nada*, "everything and nothing". For the great mystics, God is so full of Being that he is no-thing; for the modern nihilist, being is so empty of God that it is Nothing. For the theistic mystic, nothingness is only a name for Being; for the nihilist, being is a only a name for Nothingness.

The point is simply this: without God—no, not just without God, for the author of Ecclesiastes speaks frequently of God— without *faith* in God—no, not even that, for the author has faith in God, in fact, an unquestioning faith: never does he doubt God's existence—rather, without the kind of faith in God that is larger than life and therefore worth dying for and therefore worth living for, without a faith that means trust and hope and love, without a lived love affair with God, life is vanity of vanities, the shadow of a shadow, a dream within a dream.

Let me put the point in a single word. It is a word that I guarantee will shock and offend you, though it comes from Saint Paul. Paul used this word to describe his life without Christ, his life full of worldly successes, education, wealth, power, prestige, and privilege. Paul was "a Pharisee of the Pharisees", a Roman citizen, educated by Gamaliel, "the light of Israel". But before Christ put him into the post-Ecclesiastes relationship with God, what was his life? Shit. "Dung"—that was his word for it, not mine. Look up Philippians 3:8 in the bold old King James version. Compared with the all-excelling knowledge of God in Christ Jesus, all of the greatest things in this world, according to Paul, are *skubala*—shit. Dung. Job's dung heap.

That is the message of Ecclesiastes, for a Christian. The world's purest gold is only dung without Christ. But with Christ, the basest metal is transformed into the purest gold. The hopes of alchemy can come true, but on a spiritual level, not a chemical one. There is a "philosopher's stone" that transmutes all things into gold. Its name is Christ. With him, poverty is riches, weakness is power, suffering is joy, to be despised is glory. Without him, riches are poverty, power is impotence, happiness is misery, glory is despised.

This is life's greatest paradox. Solomon does not know its positive half, but he knows its negative half better than anyone.

Surprisingly, this is also the message of the most famous and adamant atheist in twentieth-century literature, especially in his first and greatest work. The writer is Sartre, and the work is *Nausea* (*La Nausée*), and the title tells it all. We cannot be too thankful to the great atheists; they show us the shape of God by his absence more clearly and starkly than believers do by his presence—like a silhouette. They show us what difference God makes as death shows us what difference life makes. You never fully appreciate a thing until it is taken away from you.

Sartre says, in "Existentialism and Humanism",

God does not exist and . . . we have to face all the consequences of this. The existentialist is strongly opposed to a certain kind of secular ethics which would like to abolish God with the least possible expense. . . . The existentialist, on the contrary, thinks it very distressing that God does not exist, because all possibility of finding values in a heaven of ideas disappears with Him; there can be no a priori Good since there is no infinite and perfect consciousness to think it. Nowhere is it written that the Good exists, that we must be honest, that we must not lie; because the fact is, we are on a plane where there are only men. Dostoyevski said, "If God didn't exist, everything would be permissible." That is the very starting point of existentialism . . . and as a result man is forlorn, because neither within him nor without does he find anything to cling to . . . if God does not exist, we find no values or commands to turn to which legitimize our conduct.

Short-Range Meanings—Enough?

Of course not all of life is in vain in the short run. Solomon knows that as well as anyone. It is not in vain to eat: it keeps you alive. It is not in vain to copulate: it keeps the human race alive and gives pleasure. It is not in vain to scratch a mosquito bite: it relieves the itching for a moment. But only for a moment. Aye, there's the rub. Short-run purpose is no compensation for long-range purposelessness.

Many think it is. "Live for the moment." Who needs a summum bonum except philosophers?

But we are all philosophers, unless we are animals. Men live not just in the present but also in the future. We live by hope. Our hearts are a beat ahead of our feet. Half of us is already in the future; we meet ourselves coming at us from up ahead. Our lives are like an arc stretching out to us from the future into the present. Our hopes and ideals move our present lives. Animals' lives are like an arc coming to them out of their past; they are determined by their past. They are pushed; we are pulled. They are forced; we are free. They are only instinct, heredity, and environment; we are more; we are persons.

The determinists, from Marx and Freud to Skinner, who deny this fact, insult us infinitely more than any preacher who shouts sin and damnation at us. It is a great compliment to call a man a sinner. Only a free man can be a sinner. The determinists mean to steal from us the great treasure of sin. They deny us our freedom, and therefore our hope, our ability to live not just from our determined past but also from our undetermined future.

Short-range meanings, long-range meaninglessness; present purposes, future purposelessness; hope about things, hopelessness about Everything—such is Ecclesiastes' picture of our lives. We are like the little black boxes you buy in joke shops. Their purpose is simply to light up, blink, make funny little noises, and shake until the batteries wear out (death). Another version has a lid; when you turn the "off/on" lever on, the box shakes, whines, blinks, and opens its lid; a little green hand comes out, shuts the box off, and falls back inside. (Same thing.) Each part of the box is meaningful; each rivet, cog, and wire is there for a purpose. But the whole thing is utterly meaningless. That is an exact image of human life according to the wisest man in the world.

No wonder we dare not read his book honestly and open-mindedly. No wonder we shake our heads, tch our tchs, and turn away. But a little black worry has been planted in our unconscious, like a bug. Might it be *true*? It *cannot* be! But is it?

Here is another image for the same point. (A picture is worth a thousand words. Jesus hardly ever spoke without using them.) It is an old Mutt and Jeff cartoon. Jeff is standing next to a pile of stones with a lit lantern on top, in the middle of a road, at night. Mutt comes along, sizes up the situation, and asks, "Jeff, did you put that lantern there?" "Yes, Mutt." "Why?" "To warn the cars away, so they wouldn't crack up on the stones." "Oh. And did you put the stones there, too?" "Yes, Mutt." "Why?" "To hold the lantern up, of course."

Sit next to a bridge in a city for a while, until the traffic over the bridge drums itself into your soul and it seems as if the bridge is inevitable and was always there. Then suddenly ask the philosophical question: Why is it there? Answer: to get people from the suburbs into the city in the morning and back out to their homes in the evening. All right, why do they go into the city? To work. At what? All sorts of meaningful jobs. For instance? Policeman, nurse, financier, construction worker, engineer, politician, shoemaker, math teacher . . . And what do these people do? Policemen police bridge traffic. Nurses heal people injured in bridge traffic. Financiers finance bridge building. Construction workers build bridges. Engineers design bridges. Politicians authorize the building of bridges. Shoemakers make shoes for crossing bridges. Math teachers educate future engineers . . . You see? The stones are there for the lantern; the lantern is there for the stones. It is the little black box, only with many more gears. But we do not notice this enormous absence. Our headphones keep us so filled with artificial noise that we do not hear the deafening silence at the heart of it all. Our heads are filled, but our hearts are empty. If we dared to listen to "the sounds of silence", like the existentialists, we would be terrified like them. Where the ancients heard cosmic music, "the music of the spheres", we hear Pascal's "eternal silence of those infinite spaces [that] fills me with dread". But we need to hear that silence. We need it more than anything else in the world. Kierkegaard wrote, "If I could prescribe just one remedy for all the ills of the modern world, I would prescribe silence. For even if the word of God were proclaimed in the modern world, no one would hear it; there is too much noise. Therefore create silence."

Ecclesiastes creates silence.

Ecclesiastes is the first and necessary step toward salvation for the modern world. The world will not go to the Great Physician (except on its own, patronizing terms) until it admits that it is desperately sick. "They that are sick need a physician, not those that are well. I came not to call the righteous, but sinners, to repentance."

Ecclesiastes is the book we moderns fear more than any other. For it is a mirror that shows us a great hole, a black spot, where our heart ought to be. The microcosm of the self has a Black Hole just like the macrocosm of the universe. What could be more terrifying than this?—to find there at our heart, where the source of life ought to be, instead the source of death?

For meaninglessness ("vanity") is the source of death. There is a death worse than death: the death of the soul; and "dead souls" (Gogol's terrifying title) can be seen on any city street. "Vanity" is death indeed; eternalized, it is Hell. Mystics and resuscitated patients who claim to catch a glimpse of Hell do not say they saw physical fire or demons with pitchforks but rather lost souls wandering nowhere in the darkness, with no direction, hope, or purpose. It is a far more terrifying picture of Hell than fire and brimstone. And, most horrible of all, it is true. It is here. We can smell those fires even now and gag on their ashes that drift into our lives.

Walker Percy suggests that the root of violence, especially rape and murder, is this sense of inner emptiness, the perception of ourselves as wraiths, ghosts. The desperate need to assure ourselves of our own reality explodes in two obvious ways: no ghost can create or destroy life by force. No ghost can rape or murder.

Children "act out" their emptiness by destructive behavior. And today's warring gangs become tomorrow's warring nations. What happens when you give adolescent gangs nuclear weapons?

The media is our drug pusher. It exploits our souls, at our command. (It is our servant; we can no more blame it than the murderer can blame his gun.) It makes its money off our addictions to death: violence, rape, murder, promiscuity, crime, drugs, and alcohol. For example, a study found that only two out of twenty recent movies took a critical rather than a positive or humorous attitude toward drugs or alcohol.

Is all this moralizing off target, a tangent from Ecclesiastes? No, it is the presence of Ecclesiastes in our lives, our own "vanity of vanities", our "Vanity Fair", a fair of fair vanities, a circus of dressed-up clowns ("Laugh, clown, laugh!"), an unmerry merry-go-round. Ecclesiastes is a terror to modern man because when he looks into its mirror he sees the ultimate nightmare: The Man With No Face.

The Great Cover-Up

All toil, all that we do, all human pursuits here "under the sun", all civilization, all arts and sciences, come down in the end for most people most of the time to a forgetting, a diversion, a cover-up: a series of complex masks over this one simple terrifying truth. Ecclesiastes rips off the cover and plunges our squeamish and reluctant eyes into this blinding abyss. It is a revelation in the literal sense: a revealing, an unveiling, an uncovering. Ecclesiastes blows our cover. The world is wise to cover up this truth by a million diversions and pretenses, for it is the most terrible truth there is. That is because once you admit it, you are at a crossroads, and only two roads lead anywhere from that crossroads. One leads to the kind of religion the world can never be comfortable with and never understand: the kind that is big enough to fill the infinite hole in the human heart, the kind bigger than life itself. The other road leads to a bullet hole through the head, the mirror image of the hole through the heart.

Five Ways to Hide an Elephant

This is not only Solomon's view of our lives; it is also the modern world's. For the modern world has no answer to the biggest and most obvious question of all: What is it all there for? What are we here for?

The question is as big as an elephant. How can you hide an elephant? The modern world has invented five ways.

1. *Diversion* is the first and most effective way to hide the elephant. An elephant can be hidden by mice, if there are enough of them. So our world is full of thousands of little things, which keep us diverted from the one big thing. We are kept so busy that we have no time to think.

2. *Propaganda* is the next. Since the modern world has no answer to the greatest of all questions, it calls it nasty names, like "abstract" and "metaphysical" and even "religious", and above all "a matter of private opinion" (and do not impose yours on me, please. That would be propaganda! No. *That* is propaganda.)—as if the nature of the real world and of our efforts to find the truth about the life we all share in this world were only a dream or a private fantasy in our own minds.

3. *Indifference* is a third way to hide an elephant. Someone

says, "There's an elephant!" and we simply yawn. There is God, or there is Nothingness; in either case, there is Death. These are three elephants, and we care more about mice. We are passionate about money and sex and ambition and indifferent to what it all means. We are specialists—nose to the switch or gear or specialized part of our little black box, indifferent to the whole and the why.

4. *The pursuit of happiness*, which our American Declaration of Independence calls one of our great, inalienable rights and which Malcolm Muggeridge calls one of the silliest ideas ever propagated, hides the elephant because the elephant does not seem to make us happy. The elephant is "negative", and we should practice "the power of positive thinking", "I'm OK, you're OK", and "self-acceptance". We should cry "Peace! Peace!" when there is no peace, because it makes us happy. "Yes, Virginia, there is a Santa Claus", and no, Virginia, people do not die, they only "pass away", and no, Virginia, all religious educators agree that the biblical "fear of the Lord" is *not* the beginning of wisdom but a dangerous superstition that must be eradicated from the minds of the young lest they become something other than well-adjusted citizens of the Kingdom of This World.

5. Finally, the reigning philosophical orthodoxy of *subjectivism* blunts the pin that could prick the balloon of happiness, namely, the pin of truth, by turning its point back upon itself: truth is what you believe, "true for you" but not for me. The best way of all to hide an elephant is to hide your eyes instead, to play peek-a-boo and not to peek, to grow ingrown eyeballs. Thus we turn the question "What is the real summum bonum; what is the truth about the good?" into the question "What is *my* set of values, my order of priorities for my life?" We reduced "the Good" to "value", "value" to "values", and "values" to "my values". And ethics is then reduced to "values clarification". Then we dare to say to an honest scientist of life like Solomon (or Moses or Saint Paul) "What right do you have to impose your values on me?"

Why do we say such nonsense? Why do we turn elephants into mice, cosmic truths into personal preferences? Because we are terrified of elephants. Perhaps we cannot ride them; perhaps they will trample us. So we reduce their size. We do the same thing to sex, and religion, and philosophy. (There are many elephants in our jungle; we have not yet succeeded in caging them all, in "demythologizing" our whole world; *Brave New World* is still a generation or two away.)

The Obscene Syllogism

What I shall now do is almost obscene. I shall put this horror—this thing that is so awful that we have to cover it up—into a nice, clean, perfect syllogism.
Here it is:

> All "toil" is "under the sun".
> And all "under the sun" is "vanity".
> Therefore, all "toil" is "vanity".

Like every syllogism, this one has three terms: (1) "toil", (2) "under the sun", and (3) "vanity".

We have already seen what "vanity" means: the Great Void, ultimate meaninglessness.

"Toil" means not just "hard work" but *any* work, everything we do, all human pursuits here "under the sun", all of human life's efforts at meaning, every life-style, every value, every candidate for the summum bonum. Solomon will experiment with five candidates, five efforts, five "toils", the five most universal and popular life-styles—wisdom, pleasure, power and riches, altruism, and conventional naturalistic religion—and he will show that each one is equally "vain".

Finally, "under the sun". (How often modern translations of the Bible rob us of great and memorable images, of poetic grandeur! I hope your Bible has preserved this great phrase.) It means simply the observed nature of the world, the way things are, "just the facts, ma'am". Solomon's mental camera takes many pictures onto his verbal photographic plate, and five recurrent features stand out in all of them: sameness, death, time, evil, and mystery. Each of these features contributes to the total vanity. Each is another reason why every "toil" is vain. Toiling under the sun is trying to find a straight road in a round world, trying to find an absolute in a relative world, trying to find an end in a "world without end". Since (1) all "toil" is "under the sun" (that is, all life is surrounded by the context of this real world), and since (2) everything in this world "under the sun" is in vain, it follows that (3) all toil is in vain; all life is meaningless.

Five "Toils"

"Toil" means all our attempts to find or make meaning. "Toil" means all the square pegs we shove into the round hole of "the existential vacuum"; all the marbles that we throw into the Grand Canyon of meaninglessness in a necessary but doomed attempt to fill it up; all the candidates for the presidential position of the summum bonum, the greatest good, that we nominate. But no one of them is good enough for the job. All are failures. Each "toil" lacks the "gain" we seek from it—not a "gaining" of money but a "gaining" of meaning.

Solomon mentions five such major candidates. As in any election, there are also many minor candidates running, which he does not mention. They are flashy, spacy, or "far out", and appeal only to small "lunatic fringes". A few people try to find their life's ultimate meaning in things like tying enormous patches of brightly colored plastic around large bridges or small islands or getting into the *Guinness Book of World Records* by dancing on one leg longer than anyone in human history. But for the vast majority, there are and always have been five basic candidates, at all times, places, and cultures. The five that

Solomon mentions are also the five mentioned, for example, in Hinduism's traditional "Four Wants of Man", in Plato's dialogues, in Aristotle's *Ethics*, in Augustine's *Confessions*, in Boethius' *Consolation of Philosophy*, in Aquinas' "Treatise on Happiness" in the *Summa*, in Kierkegaard's *Stages on Life's Way* and *Either/Or*, in Freud's *Civilization and Its Discontents*, in Sartre's *Nausea*, and in the novels of writers like Dostoyevski, Hermann Hesse, Thomas Mann, and Albert Camus. Most important of all, they are the five candidates we find ourselves and our neighbors in "real life" pursuing most of the time. They are:

1. wisdom
2. pleasure
3. wealth and power
4. duty, altruism, social service, or honor
5. piety, religion

in other words, a life of

1. philosophy to fill your mind
2. hedonism to fill your body
3. materialism to fill your pocket
4. ethics to fill your conscience
5. religion to fill your spirit

The first three constitute what Kierkegaard calls "the aesthetic stage" of life: self-satisfaction. (He classifies even speculative philosophy as "aesthetic", the satisfaction of curiosity.) The fourth is "the ethical", and the fifth he calls "religiousness A", religiousness in general as distinct from Christianity. I exist for myself in the first three, for others in the fourth, and for God in the fifth.

Solomon has tried each of these five and found them wanting both in meaningfulness and in happiness, both in objective and in subjective fullness. And he tells us why. He does not merely argue; he experiments. He lives five lives and shares with us the fruits of experience. "Don't knock it if you haven't tried it", someone may object, but Solomon has tried it all. "I have seen everything", he says. He has a perfect right to knock it all; he has seen it all.

Even religion fails Solomon, as we shall see, because it is only Kierkegaard's "religiousness A", only conventional natural religion, not supernatural revelation.

1. Wisdom

Solomon's question, remember, is the greatest of all questions: What is the greatest thing? What is the summum bonum, the ultimate end, point, goal, value, or purpose of human life on earth? What is the meaning of life? What is true success, true fulfillment, true happiness? How can I avoid getting A's in all my subjects and flunking life?

As a philosopher, Solomon naturally hopes that it will be wisdom, for philosophy is the love of wisdom. He gives us the story of this attempt and its resultant failure in Ecclesiastes 1:12–18:

> I the Preacher have been king over Israel in Jerusalem. And I applied my mind to seek and to search out by wisdom all that is done under heaven; it is an unhappy business that God has given to the sons of men to be busy with. I have seen everything that is done under the sun; and behold, all is vanity and a striving after wind. . . .
>
> I said to myself, "I have acquired great wisdom, surpassing all who were over Jerusalem before me; and my mind has had great experience of wisdom and knowledge." And I applied my mind to know wisdom and to know madness and folly. I perceived that this also is but a striving after wind. "For in much wisdom is much vexation, and he who increases knowledge increases sorrow" (Eccl 1:12–14, 16–18).

We see the dark cloud approaching in verse 13, when Solomon mentions the "unhappy business" that is the search for wisdom. "Sadder but wiser" is a common coupling. Even Socrates knew that when he said, "Is not the pursuit of wisdom a practice of death?" "Philosophizing is a rehearsal [*meletē*] for dying."

A second dark cloud comes when we hear the words "I have seen everything that is done under the sun". Only God can endure that sight; only eternity can see everything without being bored. Worse than even sorrow is boredom. Sorrow is not necessarily "vain"; boredom is.

Solomon's great quest for wisdom was not naïve or one-sided, for he studied "madness and folly" also. The terrible thing about the result of his experiments with wisdom and with folly was that both seemed to have the same result; both seemed to be a "striving after wind". Philosophy seemed as foolish as folly.

The only wisdom Solomon learned from this experiment was that "in much wisdom is much vexation, and he who increases knowledge increases sorrow". He is not the first to find this bitter water in the well of wisdom, nor the last. Think of all the people you know. Is it not true that the ones who laugh the loudest and the most are usually the shallowest and the most foolish? And that the wisest are usually the gravest? Perhaps the wise are grave because they remember the grave.

2. Pleasure

Well, if the highbrow does not have life's secret, perhaps the lowbrow has. If the mind cannot make me happy, then perhaps the body can. If one life-style fails, let us try another, an opposite one.

Pleasure is the simplest, easiest, most obvious, and most promising answer to the problem of happiness. For "happiness" seems almost to *mean* "pleasure". And pleasures are close at hand, easy to enjoy, unlike wisdom, which is a far and lofty goal, the road to which is hard to travel. Wisdom is a mountaintop; pleasure is a plain. Wisdom is mysterious; pleasure is plain. Wisdom is a walking stick; pleasure is a plane.

But one thing pleasure is not, even for Solomon, even for

the man who had it all—especially for the man who had it all—it is not meaning.

To those of us who do *not* "have it all", pleasure beckons promisingly. "The grass is always greener in the other fellow's yard." That is one of the worst things about poverty: it is deceptive. When you have little, you can still believe the lie that more will make you happy. But "poor little rich man" Solomon had it all, and the bubble burst; the illusion was shattered. The rich know from experience that riches do not make them happy; the poor can still believe this lie. That is the chief advantage of riches: not that they make you happy but that they make you *un*happy—but wise.

Solomon's experiment with pleasure lacked nothing. He had wine, women, and song; gardens, pools, slaves, cattle—a veritable Disneyland of amusements. And like with any amusement park, the fascination soon wore off.

I said to myself, "Come now, I will make a test of pleasure; enjoy yourself." But behold, this also was vanity. I said of laughter, "It is mad," and of pleasure, "What use is it?" I searched with my mind how to cheer my body with wine—my mind still guiding me with wisdom—and how to lay hold on folly, till I might see what was good for the sons of men to do under heaven during the few days of their life. I made great works; I built houses and planted vineyards for myself; I made myself gardens and parks, and planted in them all kinds of fruit trees. I made myself pools from which to water the forest of growing trees. I bought male and female slaves, and had slaves who were born in my house; I had also great possessions of herds and flocks, more than any who had been before me in Jerusalem. I also gathered for myself silver and gold and the treasure of kings and provinces; I got singers, both men and women, and many concubines, man's delight.

So I became great and surpassed all who were before me in Jerusalem; also my wisdom remained with me. And whatever my eyes desired I did not keep from them; I kept my heart from no pleasure, for my heart found pleasure in all my toil, and this was my reward for all my toil. Then I considered all that my hands had done and the toil I had spent in doing it, and behold, all was vanity and a striving after wind, and there was nothing to be gained under the sun (Eccl 2:1–11).

Every serious hedonist knows the result of the experiment: pleasure inevitably becomes boring, sooner or later. In Greek philosophy, the pursuit of pleasure soon turned into the pursuit of *apatheia*, apathy, the avoidance of pain and passion. In modern times, the pursuit of pleasure often turns into an addiction: stronger and stronger doses must be found to fend off the familiarity and boredom. Sometimes it becomes, bizarrely, its opposite: the pursuit of pain, sadomasochism— anything to relieve the boredom.

Hedonists are suckers for salesmen. They are in the market for anything—anything that might relieve the boredom. That is why hedonism and materialism are bedfellows: an addict has no sales resistance.

3. Power

Power is a deeper desire than pleasure, though most of us do not realize this. This is Adler's improvement on Freud's "pleasure principle". Kierkegaard explains why: "If I had a servant in my employ who, when I asked him for a cup of cold water, brought instead the world's costliest wines blended in a chalice, I would dismiss him; for true pleasure consists not in getting my wine but in getting my way."

If we have power, we can push the pleasure buttons at will. Power is broader than pleasure because it includes power over pleasure.

We are more threatened by loss of power and control than by loss of pleasure; by a little inconvenience that we cannot control, like a torn nylon or a car that will not start, than by a great inconvenience that we make voluntarily, under our own power. A little pain bothers us more than a great one if it is not freely chosen. We willingly, even happily, run through the rain to the store to get there before it closes to buy a cup of coffee for the one we love. Our tired muscles and sweating body are offered up as loving martyrdom. But let an insensitive boss command the same act from us, and we will curse him at every step of the way.

Augustine, in the *Confessions*, goes so far as to find the deepest and darkest motive for sin in the desire to be like God in power, to be over the moral law rather than under it. Why did he steal those hard, bitter pears when he was sixteen? Why did Adam and Eve eat the forbidden fruit? To be "like God". But, as Aquinas says, if we are like God in power but not in goodness, then we are not even like God in power, because God's power is one with his goodness.

No Jew except Jesus ever wielded greater power than Solomon. He was Israel's most absolute monarch. His reign was at the top of the mountain of Israel's history. Never before or since has there been such military, economic, and territorial power and wealth. Yet this too was vanity.

Solomon does not describe his experiment with power as one clearly distinct from his experiment with pleasure, but as a part of it (Eccl 2:8). The form his power took was wealth, the most obvious form of power. Wealth can buy everything that money can buy. Unfortunately, it cannot buy a single thing that money cannot buy: meaning, purpose, happiness, peace, or love.

But from the very failure of power we can find a deep clue to success. Power tries to control things and succeeds, but it cannot buy or control meaning. Meaning, therefore, is not something we can control. It must be free. It must be gift. It must be love.

But wait. We are going too fast. That answer does not come in this book but in another. We must fully understand the problem before we can fully understand the solution. So for the sake of fully understanding love, let us not yet think about love.

4. *Ethics*

Solomon takes a great leap forward when he abandons the threefold pursuit of selfish gain, satisfying his mind, his body, or his pocketbook, and embarks on a fourth and very different experiment: altruism, philanthropy, social service, working for others, especially for posterity. This vastly expands his horizon, his spirit, and his chance to find meaning.

> Two are better than one, because they have a good reward for their toil. For if they fall, one will lift up his fellow; but woe to him who is alone when he falls and has not another to lift him up. Again, if two lie together, they are warm; but how can one be warm alone? And though a man might prevail against one who is alone, two will withstand him. A threefold cord is not quickly broken (Eccl 4:9–11).

But even this is not enough, and that is perhaps the most shocking lesson of all to the typically modern counterpart who assumes that of course a life of service to neighbor is the highest wisdom, the greatest good, and the definitive and self-sufficient answer to the problem of vanity. The reason it is not enough is quite simple. All Solomon has found so far are vain toys. How can the gift of vanity be more than vain? If wisdom, pleasure, wealth, and power were vain for him, they will be equally vain for those with whom he shares them. Multiply zero by any number and you still get only zero. If you do not know what the meaning of life is, how can you find it by leading others to it? We all know what happens when the blind lead the blind: both fall into the pit. It is all very well to prefer altruism to egotism, to work for the good of others, but what *is* the good of others? Once I find the summum bonum, it must be shared, yes, but I cannot share it before I find it.

And, as Solomon sagely puts it, what good does it do to work for posterity if posterity is a fool? "I hated all my toil in which I had toiled under the sun, seeing that I must leave it to the man who will come after me; and who knows whether he will be a wise man or a fool? Yet he will be master of all for which I toiled" (Eccl 2:18–19).

5. Conventional religion

True religion would indeed be big enough to fill the hole in Solomon's heart. But Solomon's religion is conventional religion, not true religion. The true knowledge of God is the answer, the only adequate answer, to the greatest problem in the world. But Solomon's God is only the God of the Enlightenment, the God of reason, and this God is far too small.

Solomon is honest. In a sense that is his undoing. He does not fake it; he knows that the God of nature and human reason alone, the God known only by observation and experience under the sun, is little more than an x, an unknown quantity, a vague First Cause, the one who stands invisibly behind everything. Aye, there's the rub—everything. Evil as well as good. God, like the universe, does not seem to give a damn: "In the day of prosperity be joyful, and in the day of adversity consider; God has made the one as well as the other, so that men may not find out anything that will be after him" (Eccl 7:14).

Such a God could be believed and feared but hardly loved or trusted. Such a God is not Abba, Father, Daddy, but merely a "father figure", the absent father, "the Great White Father". Such a God is merely "the Force" of *Star Wars*.

Observation of nature shows no divine preference for the good guys. Innocent little bunny rabbits and human babies do not fare well against predatory coyotes or leukemia. Observation of human life is no better: the good die young, and the better you are, the more likely it is that you will be martyred. We men have a penchant for assassinating our heroes as well as our villains, our very good men and our very bad men (men, seldom women so far, though if the radical feminists have their way, the women will soon be as present on both bloody ends of the assassin's gun as the men have been). The safest course in such a world, Solomon sees, is: "Be not righteous overmuch . . . why should you destroy yourself? And be not wicked overmuch . . . why should you die before your time?" (Eccl 7:16–17).

Such a religion is as dull as the world. It is superfluous. Such a God is merely there, not here; an it, not an I; a thing to acknowledge, not a person to love and listen to and long for. The Great Unknown, however great, cannot fill the hole in our heart or the hole in our head. He must become known. But that story is in the rest of the Bible.

All five candidates for the position of the summum bonum, all five "toils" under the sun, all five of the things men hope in and give their hearts and lives to, have proved vain. The reason is that they are all under the sun, and everything under the sun is vain. Why?

Five Vanities

Solomon gives five reasons for his major premise, that everything "under the sun" is vain. He observes five features of this world and life "under the sun" that make it all vain. All five are omnipresent. Like cancers, they extend their tendrils into every corner of our lives. Any one of these five cancers would be enough to kill meaning; life is infected with all five of them. They are:

1. the sameness and indifference of all things
2. death as the certain and final end of life
3. time as a cycle of endless repetition
4. evil as the perennial and unsolvable problem
5. God as an unknowable mystery

1. Sameness and indifference

We make value judgments. We prefer one thing to another: life to death, beauty to ugliness, good to evil. Nature does not. Nature is indifferent. In the words of Stephen Crane,

> A man said to the universe,
> Sir, I exist!
> Nevertheless, replied the universe,
> That fact has not created in me
> The slightest feeling of obligation.

Take a Gallup poll of the universe. Ask it how many organisms it has brought into life. Let the answer be x. Now ask it how many of these organisms it has brought back to death or is in the process of bringing to death. The number will again be x. Not $x+1$, not $x-1$, but x. The universe has no preferences. We do. We do not fit this universe. The great tragedy of life is not just that bad things happen but that bad things happen to good people exactly as frequently as to bad people. The tragedy is that

> everything . . . is vanity, since one fate comes to all, to the righteous and the wicked, to the good and the evil, to the clean and to the unclean, to him who sacrifices and him who does not sacrifice (Eccl 9:1–2).

> Again I saw that under the sun the race is not to the swift, nor the battle to the strong, nor bread to the wise, nor riches to the intelligent [that's for sure!], nor favor to men of skill, but time and chance happen to them all (Eccl 9:11).

The universe seems exactly like Rhett Butler in *Gone with the Wind*. This is the face it turns on us: "Frankly, my dear, I just don't give a damn."

2. Death

Death is the most inconvenient thing in life, but also the most obvious—like an elephant in your kitchen. It is also the strongest reason why life seems vain. What profit is there in an investment in any of a country's businesses if the country is about to be destroyed?

But death is now. As soon as we are born, we begin to die. We are all equally bankrupt, some of us not yet declared: the small and arrogant oligarchy of the living, surrounded by the far more populous democracy of the dead.

What is the meaning of death? Here is all that human reason based on observation of life here under the sun can answer:

> The fate of the sons of men and the fate of beasts is the same; as one dies, so dies the other. . . . All go to one place; all are from the dust and all turn to dust again. Who knows whether the spirit of man goes upward and the spirit of the beast goes down to the earth? (Eccl 3:19–21).

Who knows, indeed? Here under the sun, no one. Unless there should appear here under the sun a man who came from beyond the sun, beyond the horizon of death's night—unless we saw the Rising Son. But Solomon had not yet seen that man, only the man of dust, "from the earth, earthly", not the man from heaven; and what he says about the man of dust, the first Adam and all his descendants, is simply true. As Pascal put it in the *Pensées*, "the ending is dreary, however fine the rest of the play. They put a little dirt over your head, and that is the end, forever. That is the end awaiting the world's most illustrious life."

Alexander the Great is said to have directed that he be buried with his naked arm hanging out of his coffin, with his hand empty, to show the world that the man who conquered the world left it as he entered it: naked. "Naked I came from my mother's womb; naked I return." Underneath our temporary life-clothing, we are all death-naked.

As an argument takes its point from its conclusion, so a story takes its point from its ending. If death is, as it seems to be, the final end, then life's story is vanity with a vengeance. The cosmos has been groaning in evolutionary travail with us, and we are only the cosmic abortion.

3. Time

Time is vanity because "time is just another word for death".
Time is a river that takes from us everything it gives us.
Nothing remains; time ravages the very stars.

Is there progress? Does time go anywhere? Are we in a
story? Not if observation under the sun tells us the truth about
time. For such observation sees only cycles, "a time to be born
and a time to die . . . a time to plant and a time to pluck up
what is planted. . . . What gain has the worker from his toil?"
(Eccl 3:2, 9). There is "nothing new under the sun". There is no
good news, no Gospel. Progress is a myth, and evolution, if
not another myth, is only a temporary segment of a vaster
cosmic process, the "up" side of the cycle. Entropy is the
"down" side. The myth of progress is like believing you are
climbing a mountain just because you are going up an anthill
on the way down.

If time is vain, life is vain, for all of life is temporal. Time is
the fundamental and ineradicable feature of all our experience
under the sun, spiritual as well as physical, for it takes time to
think as well as to act; our souls are in time just as our bodies
are, though not in space. Yet despite this ubiquitous and
inescapable vanity of time there is one light of hope, one chink
in the forbidding wall, one verse where Solomon opens a
window out onto another world, like the poet's "casements
opening on perilous foam" of "faerie lands forlorn". After
bemoaning time's meaningless cycles, he says, about God, "he
has made everything beautiful [that is, fitting] for its time, but
he has also put eternity into man's mind [or heart, or spirit]."
We experience only time, yet we desire eternity, timelessness.
Why, for Heaven's sake? Where did we ever learn of this thing
called eternity, to desire it? Why, if our existence is totally
environed by time, do we not feel at home in it? "Do fish
complain of the sea for being wet?" Yet we complain of time.
There is never enough time for anything. Time, our natural
environment, is our enemy.

Perhaps there is land. Perhaps we were not always fish or will not always be. Perhaps—more than perhaps. Innate desires bespeak real objects. If there is hunger, there is food. And there is an innate hunger for eternity.

But this food is not found under the sun. Solomon shows us, by contrast, what and where the meaning of life is by showing what and where it is not. It is Yonder. There is More. There are more things in Heaven and earth than are dreamed of in all our philosophies. That is the announcement of hope. Hope's messenger has infiltrated even into the castle of doom. Our desire for eternity, our divine discontent with time, is hope's messenger.

4. Evil

The problem of evil, of injustice, of the sufferings of the innocent, of bad things happening to good people, is the oldest of all puzzles and the strongest of all arguments against belief in the goodness of God and the goodness of life.

> There is a vanity which takes place on earth, that there are righteous men to whom it happens according to the deeds of the wicked, and there are wicked men to whom it happens according to the deeds of the righteous . . . (Eccl 8:14).

> Moreover, I saw under the sun that in the place of justice, even there was wickedness (Eccl 3:16).

> Again I saw all the oppressions that are practiced under the sun. And behold, the tears of the oppressed, and they had no one to comfort them. On the side of their oppressors was power, and there was no one to comfort them! (Eccl 4:1).

The poor and oppressed you will always have with you, Jesus said. Twenty centuries have not solved the problem, nor will twenty more. Time does not solve evil. Nothing under the sun does.

Even a little evil seems to destroy a lot of good: "Dead flies make the perfumer's ointment give off an evil odor; so a little folly outweighs wisdom and honor." One bull in a china shop, one madman's finger on a machine gun or a nuclear button, one ill-chosen word, one infidelity, can ruin a whole life. Good is hostage to evil. This too is vanity.

5. God

Is meaning in God, then?

Yes, but not in Solomon's God. Not in the God known by unaided reason. Not in "nature and nature's God". That is simply an it, not a who, a piece of celestial machinery called the First Cause or Great Architect or unknown Designer behind nature's known design. If all we know about God is what we read from nature, we shall conclude five things:

1. that God exists;
2. that God is powerful enough to make the world;
3. that God is intelligent enough to design the world;
4. perhaps also that God is aesthetic enough to create the beauty of the world, a great work of art;
5. but not that God is good, loving, or even just or that he cares about us and our lives. There is no evidence under the sun for that, the thing we really care about, the thing that would make God not just "the Force" but the Father. We are terrified little children, "lost in a haunted wood", and we need Abba, Daddy, not a Force or First Cause. We need a God whose name is not x but I.

This Solomon is not a fool. Therefore he has not said in his heart, "There is no God." But this Solomon is also not a child of God. God is not his Father but his blank, his Unknown:

"Consider the work of God: Who can make straight what he has made crooked?"

The God of nature lets brain tumors appear in little babies' heads. The most pious possible reactions to that fact are agnosticism and intellectual humility:

Then I saw all the work of God, that man cannot find out the work that is done under the sun. However much man may toil in seeking, he will not find it out; even though a wise man claims to know, he cannot find it out . . . (Eccl 8:17).

As you do not know how the spirit comes to the bones in the womb of a woman with child, so you do not know the work of God who makes everything (Eccl 11:5).

Is it possible to believe in God and still despair, still not know why you are living? Certainly. Solomon does. For his God is like the moon: there, but not here, controlling the tides of his life but not entering into any personal relationship with him, no face-to-face encounter as with Job. Solomon's God has no face; he is only Being, only Am, not I Am. For Solomon's epistemology is purely naturalistic, and nature is only God's back. But Scripture is God's mouth, and Jesus is God's face. Ecclesiastes is a perfect silhouette of Jesus, the stark outline of the darkness that the face of Jesus fills.

The Need for an Answer: Three Demonic Doors

It is essential that we escape Ecclesiastes' conclusion somehow. It is essential, in an absolute and unqualified way, that vanity be refuted, that the most horrible of all demons be exorcised.

There are three doors by which this demon can enter our lives. There is an emotional, psychological door, connected with depression. There is also a central door, a spiritual door, which has no name but is the opposite of faith. Its name is not doubt, for great faith can coexist with great doubt, as in Job. Nor is it simply unfaith, not-yet-faith, for that can be seeking, and "all who seek, find". Rather, it is a kind of antifaith such as we see in great atheists like Sartre and Nietzsche, who care as much about God's unreality as the great saints care about

God's reality. There is also a third door, a rational, intellectual, philosophical, argumentative, reason-giving door. And that is the door Ecclesiastes opens.

It is equally necessary to bar all three doors. Psychology has its bar for the first door. Religion has its far greater bar for the second, far greater door, the central door. But philosophy too must have its bar for its door, the third door. Each bar is different. Psychology cannot use philosophy's bar, rational arguments, to fight depression. Religion cannot use mere psychological techniques to heal souls, though our age is full of fools who try. Psychologists can remove guilt feelings, but only God can remove real guilt. And philosophy cannot bar its door with nonrational, nonphilosophical bars, whether those bars are subrational, superrational, or simply nonrational. Even if religious faith is far greater than reason, it is not a substitute for reason. And we are commanded by our faith itself to "be ready to give a reason for the hope that is in you".

No one *wants* to admit Solomon's conclusion that "all is vanity". But we cannot simply assert that we disbelieve it. Solomon has given us some very good reasons for believing it. He has built a strong case, a strong building. We must undermine it. We must refute his argument.

I think God providentially arranged for this book to be in the Bible for that express purpose. God is practicing "Socratic method" on us, giving us a question, a challenge, and demanding that *we* give the answer, the response. Life does that to us. We keep asking life, "What is your meaning?" and life responds by throwing challenges at us that demand that we respond to them. Life asks *us*, "What is *your* meaning?" Adam, after the Fall, wondered where God was, and God, instead of answering, asked him, "Adam, where are you?" Job looked for God as his Answer Man, but when God showed up, he asked Job for *his* answers: "Now it is my turn to ask the questions and yours to answer." The mystics and resuscitated patients say that the "Being of Light" they see asks them a question, though not usually in words: something like: "Give an account of yourself. I am the Light. Stand in the light."

There is nothing more boring than an answer to a question you never asked or cared about. Most religious education is like that—most secular education, too. Unlike our human teachers, God did not make that mistake. Ecclesiastes is the question. The Bible is a diptych, a two-paneled picture. Ecclesiastes is the first panel, the question. The rest of the Bible is the second panel, the answer. The Bible is like life, like history according to Toynbee: "Challenge and response". Ecclesiastes is the challenge. The rest is the response.

Well, have we understood the response? Can we answer Ecclesiastes? Can we translate our faith into the language of reason? Can we "give a reason for the hope that is in us"?

Rules for Talking Back

When we talk back, we want to do more than just "share our feelings" or opinions. That is childish; that is just "getting it out", "getting it off our chest". We want not just to get something out but to get something *in*: the truth. We want not just to "express our opinion" but to be *im*pressed by the truth. We want not just to externalize what is inside but to internalize what is outside: to learn the truth, to find out whether Solomon speaks the truth. That is, if we are honest.

There are only three ways to refute any argument. This is not negotiable, conventional, or changeable, not the man-made rules of a man-made game. This situation is inherent in the structure of reason itself. Aristotle did not invent it; God did.

An argument—any argument—has three ingredients, and any one of these three ingredients can be defective. But there are only these three. An argument is composed of propositions, statements, sentences. These in turn are composed of terms (words or phrases). An argument is built of these building blocks, just like a physical building. Its propositions are like storys, and its terms are like rooms. Each argument is a three-story building (if it is a syllogism, the natural and most usual form of argument and the form we find in Ecclesiastes). The storys are called two "premises" and one "conclusion". The conclusion is like the top story; it is where the building *goes*. Each story has two rooms, called the "subject term" and the "predicate term". Thus a syllogistic argument looks like this:

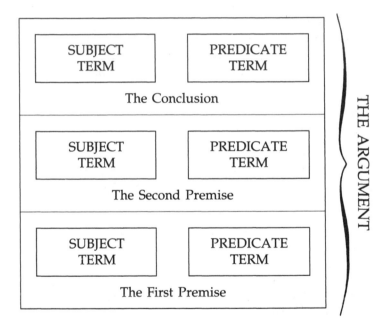

There are three things that must go right with any argument:

1. The terms must be unambiguous.
2. The premises must be true.
3. The argument must be logical.

Thus there are three things that can go wrong with any argument:

1. The terms may be ambiguous.
2. The premises may be false.
3. The argument may be illogical.

Ecclesiastes' basic argument is as follows:

> All "toil" is "under the sun".
> All "under the sun" is "vanity".
> Therefore, all "toil" is "vanity".

If we are to refute this argument, we must find in it one of the following:

1. an ambiguous term
2. a false premise
3. a logical fallacy

But no term is used ambiguously, and there is no logical fallacy—the conclusion logically follows from the premises. We must therefore find a false premise.

There are only two premises: that all toil, all human work, is under the sun, and that all that is under the sun is vanity, for the five reasons given. Well, is there a toil that is not under the sun? Is there a human work that is not confined to this earth? What are we doing here? Are we not building an eternal Kingdom? Will nothing last? William Butler Yeats writes of a little girl watching the waves destroy sand castles on a Normandie beach, thinking of all the great civilizations that had come gone in that place, and lamenting, "Will nothing last?"

But we will last. We are constructing our very selves with every choice we make, like statues sculpting their own shape with the chisel of free will. And those selves, souls, characters, are destined for eternity. We are the Kingdom of Heaven. We are the answer to Solomon. But this answer does not come clear until hundreds of years after Solomon, through the most outrageous paradox, which Kierkegaard calls "the absolute paradox", of the event of eternity entering time, God's becoming a man, sharing the life of man so that man could share the life of God. Ecclesiastes is the question to which Christ is the answer.

And the second premise—he has tried the five most popularly practiced experiments with life, but is there nothing he has not tried? Is there anything else under the sun, anything that is not in vain? The next book in the Bible, also bearing the name of Solomon, gives the answer. Solomon has tried pleasure, and nine hundred wives, but not love. In Song of Songs Solomon loves only one woman. The one can give what the many cannot give: a meaning larger than life's vanity. Love, true love, agape, charity, total self-giving, is the one thing in this life under the sun that is "stronger than death", that smells of eternity, that alone never gets boring, that is never exhausted, that becomes more fulfilling, not less, the more it is practiced. Love is infinite. For God is love. Love is also true wisdom. Fools say love is blind. But God is love; is God blind? One of those three propositions must go. In Ecclesiastes, God is not love. In Song of Songs, love is not blind.

One More Answer to Ecclesiastes: The Divine Interruption

The most ineradicable reason Solomon gives for vanity is the very nature of time itself as cyclic. And the four great divine deeds revealed in the Bible all break the cycle and introduce something radically new, something from without, outside time itself, something from eternity rather than from the past, therefore something radically new: Creation, Incarnation, Resurrection, and Last Judgment. Here is something new under the sun because it comes from beyond the sun. Here are meaning and hope, though terror too. Here is true transcendence.

The Postscript

The last six verses of Ecclesiastes, most scholars think, were added by a second author, the original book ending with verse 8 of chapter 12: exactly where it began, with "vanity of vanities, all is vanity". The second author adds the orthodox answer to Solomon's question, the answer the rest of the Old Testament gives, in the last two verses: "The end of the matter: all has been heard. Fear God and keep his commandments. For this is the whole duty of man. For God will bring every deed into judgment, with every secret thing, whether good or evil" (Eccl 12:13).

The other thirty-eight books of the Old Testament are summarized in these last two verses. Here indeed are the meaning and purpose of life. For the fear of the Lord is the beginning of wisdom. But it is not the end.

> The fear of the Lord, that is the beginning of wisdom, and therefore belongs to the beginnings, and is felt in the first cold hours before the dawn of civilization: the power that comes out of the wilderness and rides on the whirlwind and breaks the gods of stone; the power before which the eastern nations are prostrate like a pavement; the power before which the primitive prophets run naked and shouting, at once proclaiming and escaping from their god; the fear that is rightly rooted in the beginnings of every religion, true or false; the fear of the Lord, that is the beginning of wisdom; but not the end (G. K. Chesterton, *The Everlasting Man*).

Conclusion

Ecclesiastes is a bright book of life. It is bright precisely in its dazzling darkness. It is a book of life precisely because it honestly and nakedly confronts the fact of death. It is a great, great book because it explores, deeply and uncompromisingly, a great, great question: What are our lives here under the sun *for*?

That is the greatest question in the world. The only greater book than this would have to be a book that gave the greatest answer in the world—a book like the next book in the Bible, the Song of Songs. The philosopher asks the question, but the lover answers it. The head thinks, but the heart sings.

In the Song of Songs, life is seen as a love song. Our lives are notes in a great music, a cosmic harmony, a "music of the spheres", and the point of the song is love because the singer of the song is God—our story, history, is his story—and God *is* love. But that is another story. And the way to it is by way of Job.

JOB:

Life as Suffering

It is universally recognized that Job is one of the greatest books ever written: a masterpiece, an all-time classic. To the sensitive reader, it is real magic. It is terrifying and beautiful, beautifully terrifying and terrifyingly beautiful. It is fascinating, haunting, teasingly mysterious, tender, and yet powerful as a sledge-hammer. It can be obsessive as few books can.

Though bottomlessly mysterious, it is also simple and obvious in its main "lesson", which lies right on the surface in the words of God to Job at the end. Unless you are Rabbi Kushner, who incredibly manages to miss the unmissable, you cannot miss the message. If Job is about the problem of evil, then Job's answer to that problem is that *we do not know* the answer. We do not know what philosophers from Plato to Rabbi Kushner so helpfully but hopelessly try to teach us: why "bad things happen to good people". Job does not understand this fact of life, and neither do we. We "identify" with Job not in his knowledge but in his ignorance.

The book of Job is an enigma answering another enigma. The enigma it answers is life's deepest problem, the problem of evil, of suffering, of injustice in a world supposedly ruled by a just God. This God, however, is not a hard, bright, brittle, little formula but a mystery. He is the God of whom Rabbi Abraham Heschel said, "God is not nice. God is not an uncle. God is an earthquake." We may or may not like the God who is an earthquake rather than an uncle, but our likes and dislikes do not change reality. If we cannot take the God of Job (and the rest of the Bible), that is skin off our noses but not off God's. We do not make the universe hold its breath by holding ours.

Job is mystery. A mystery satisfies something in us, but not our reason. The rationalist in us is repelled by Job, as Job's three rationalist friends were repelled by Job. But something deeper in us is deeply satisfied by Job, and is nourished. Job is not like consommé, clear and bright, but like minestrone, dark and thick. It sticks to your ribs. When we read Job we are like a little child eating his spinach. "Open your mouth and close your eyes." Job, like spinach, is not sweet tasting. But it puts iron in our blood.

The power of Job is like the power of the Hebrew language itself. Max Picard described this language (in *The World of Silence*) as severely limited but concentrated in power (like a laser beam), able to say only a few things, but those few things that it says it says with a trumpet. Its words are like great columns sunk one by one into the earth. The words are vertical words; they join Heaven and earth, as the one Word of God, Jesus, was to do centuries later. Hebrew is the language of the Incarnation. There is a similar "feel" of "verticality" about Job, as if it were written in Heaven.

I would never have understood Job without the help of two very great writers: J. R. R. Tolkien and Martin Buber. Of course I still do not understand it, but now I can at least stand under it and not under something else that I confuse with it (that is mis-under-stand-ing). Tolkien is the one who translated Job for the Jerusalem Bible, and Buber is the one whose single suggestion gave me the key to open Job's most mysterious locked door. Let me briefly explain each of these two contributions.

Only once have I ever encountered a translation that made such a difference, that so opened up for me a previously closed book. That was Frank Sheed's translation of Augustine's *Confessions*, which I found to be as living as molten lava. The most widely used translation of the *Confessions* is the one by a Mr. Pine-Coffin, and it is worthy of his name. It is a dead translation. Sheed's is living. When I first read Job in the Jerusalem Bible translation, I did not know Tolkien was the translator. Then, after the remarkable experience of seeing the book open up and come to life and leap out at me from the pages, I later found out that the can opener was Tolkien, whom I always thought to be one of the great epic storytellers of all time. Surely nothing since *The Divine Comedy* can match *The Lord of the Rings* except *Paradise Lost*. Together with *The Aeneid* and *The Iliad* and *Odyssey*, these six make up an epic class of their own.

But I must thank Martin Buber even more for putting in my

hand the golden key that opened up the central door, the central theme of the book, the central solution to the central enigma. Even more than that, this key opened up one of the deepest secrets of theology for me, Christian theology as much as or even more than Buber's own Jewish theology, by illuminating the *koan* puzzle of God's own self-revealed name, the sacred Tetragrammaton, the Ultima Thule of human thought, the revelation of the nature of ultimate reality, the essential nature of God as he is in himself, not just in relation to us. All this was done in a startlingly simple, unexpectedly unsophisticated way. The key to Job is in Exodus 3:14.

But I am going too fast. I will not talk any more about this solution yet, because a solution is meaningless without an appreciation of the problem. I hope I have whetted your appetite with the promise of a spiritual meal of gourmet dimensions and with just desserts. But we must now begin at the beginning, with the enormously troubling problems raised by this book. I do not mean the problems *about* the book raised by scholars (for example, who wrote it, why, when, where, and so on) but the problems about life, that is, about ourselves, raised *by* this book. What are they?

Job is like an onion, or a set of nesting boxes, or a package wrapped in many layers. Peel off the outside, and there are more and more on the inside. It is bigger on the inside than on the outside—like a human being, and like the stable in Bethlehem, and like Mary's womb. There are surely many more problems, and levels of problems, than the four I see and say here, but these four, at least, are there, and they are a start, a priming of your pump so that you, the free and independent reader, can find more on your own.

1. The "Problem of Evil"

This is surely *the* problem, the problem of problems. Most generally, it is the problem of why there is evil at all, especially in a universe created and ruled by an all-good and all-powerful God. Aquinas formulates the problem with maximum succinctness in the *Summa*: "If one of two contraries is infinite, the other is wholly eliminated. But God is infinite goodness. Thus if God exists, evil would be wholly eliminated. But there is evil. Therefore God does not exist" (*STh* I, 2, 3, Obj. 1). Augustine's version is a little longer and a little more explicit: "If God were all-good, He would will only good, and if He were all-powerful, He would be able to do all that He wills. But there is evil [as well as good]. Therefore God is either not all-good or not all-powerful, or both." A third formulation of the problem is more practical than theoretical: How could God—the all-good and all-powerful God—let bad things happen to good people? This formulation is closer to Job's complaint. It is not just the sheer existence of evil, any evil at all, but the personal presence and experience of evil, the specific evil of injustice, that is the pressing problem. Punishment for deserved crime is evil in a sense, because punishment has to hurt, but in another sense it is not evil at all but good: it is justice. But Job is experiencing not justice but injustice. Bad things—very, very bad things—are happening to him, and he is "good people", in fact very, very "good people" according to the author of the book (Job 1:1) and, even more authoritatively, according to the author of Job's very being, God himself (Job 1:8).

There are only four possible answers to this problem. First, there is the obvious (but wrong) answer for someone who believes in the God of the Bible, the God who is both all good and all powerful: namely, that Job is not "good people". This is the answer of Job's three friends, and it is enormously reasonable. The author of the book has to go out of his way to tell the reader at the very beginning that Job is "a sound and upright man, one who fears God and turns away from evil" and to put this truth into the mouth of God himself (Job 1:8). Otherwise, like Job's three friends, we would certainly opt for this solution. The shocking contrast between appearance and reality, between what appears to be the obviously true solution and what is the real, infinitely more difficult and mysterious and surprising solution, is one of the main dramatic interests of the book. We must not see Job's three friends as fools, because they are not and because then we would miss the great drama, the irony, the contrast between appearance and reality. We must sympathize with the friends in order to be shocked by God, as they were. In a sense this is the main reason the book was written: to shock the reader with God, the real God, the "Lord of the Absurd", to use Father Raymond Nogar's title, as distinct from the comfortable and convenient God of our own expectations and categorizations. If God himself, the all-wise designer of the whole story we are in, were *not* this shocking and surprising "Lord of the Absurd" but rational, predictable, comfortable, and convenient, then life would not be a mystery to be lived but a problem to be solved, not a love story but a detective story, not a tragicomedy but a formula. For tragedy and comedy are the two primary forms of mystery, and if Job teaches us anything, it is that we are living in a mystery.

The first answer to the problem, then, the answer of Job's three friends, namely, that Job is *not* "good people", is to be rejected because (1) it is evidently not the answer of the author of Job, (2) God himself refutes this answer both at the beginning of the book when he speaks to Satan about Job's virtues and at the end when he praises Job and castigates Job's three friends, and (3) this answer would reduce life's central mystery to a problem. So we must turn to a second possible answer.

Perhaps God is not good. This is the answer Job flirts dangerously with when he dreams of dragging God to court and winning his case if there were only an impartial and just judge to sit above both himself and God, but laments that there is no such judge and that God has all the power on his side, but not justice. In other words, God is not good, but God is powerful, so goodness (justice) and power are ultimately separated, not one. This is a horrible, an unspeakably horrible, philosophy, and only Job's honesty and scepticism about his own innocence deliver him from it:

> How dare I plead my cause, then,
> Or choose arguments against him?
> Suppose I am in the right, what use is my defense?
> For he whom I must sue is judge as well.
> If he deigned to answer my citation,
> Could I be sure that he would listen to my voice?
> He, who for one hair crushes me,
> Who, for no reason, wounds and wounds again,
> Leaving me not a moment to draw breath,
> With so much bitterness he fills me.
> Shall I try force? Look how strong he is!
> Or go to court? But who will summon him?
> Though I think myself right, his mouth may condemn
>   me;
> Though I count myself innocent, it may declare me a
>   hypocrite.
> But am I innocent after all? Not even I know that,
> And, as for my life, I find it hateful.
> It is all one, and this I dare to say:
> Innocent and guilty, he destroys all alike.
> When a sudden deadly scourge descends,
> He laughs at the plight of the innocent. . . .
> Yes, I am man, and he is not; and so no argument,
> No suit between the two of us is possible.
> There is no arbiter between us
> To lay his hand on both (Job 9:14–23, 32–33).

The Resurrection of Christ fills the Christian with cosmic joy because it definitively, concretely refutes the horrible philosophy that goodness and power are ultimately separated. Goodness incarnate, the only totally good man who ever lived, the only infinitely good thing ever to appear to finite eyes, triumphed over death, the great evil power that no man can conquer, "the last enemy". The psychological consequences of belief in the Resurrection are so ingrained in the Christian consciousness that we usually do not realize the chasm between Yes and No here, between belief and unbelief. Try to imagine it: one day you realize that God does not care, that almighty power is indifferent to good and evil, that the story of the universe and the story of your life are told by a bland, blank blah instead of a loving Person. That is the horror that looms on Job's horizon here.

Denial of the Resurrection, or of the conjunction of ultimate goodness with ultimate power, can take another form, and this is a third answer to the problem of evil: instead of denying God's goodness, we can deny God's power. Imagine one day discovering the bones of the dead Jesus in a Jerusalem tomb. The logical result is the same in both cases—the phenomenon of evil is "explained"—but the psychological results are different. If the God we worship is power but not goodness, goodness is demoted and power exalted in objective reality, and therefore in our lives, too, if we are sane enough to conform our lives to objective reality. We then begin to worship power and reduce goodness to a secondary thing, a means to the end of power or success. Thus religion is divorced from ethics. If, in contrast, the God we worship is goodness but not power, we still put goodness and ethics at the highest level, as absolute, but we cannot trust or expect the good to triumph. We side with God, but we are not confident we are on the winning side. We are good but not confident. If we believe solution number two, the affirmation of God's power but not of his goodness, we are confident but not good. If we believe solution number three, the affirmation of God's goodness but not of his power, we are good but not confident.

Solution number three, the denial of God's omnipotence, is a very popular solution today, as it was in pagan times. The pagan version of it was polytheism, dividing God into little godlets, none of which has total power. The modern version of it is reducing God to nature or time (process). "Process theology" is the fashionable form of this heresy today. Rabbi

Kushner and Dr. Nicholas Woltersdorff have both recently written very popular books propounding this solution for the very same reason: each of them had to rethink his faith in light of a tragic death of a beloved teenaged son. Each had to hold on to the love of God, God as lovable, God as good. Each concluded that God was not in total control of things, that God is still growing and perhaps will always be growing and learning, that God is subject to natural laws. This means that the lovable and loving Person of God is not the ultimate, but that impersonal necessity or the laws of nature are ultimate. They are above God himself. This "solution" takes from us the precious gift of confidence and trust. We can no longer be little children, as Christ commands, and call God "Abba" ("da-da"), totally secure in his arms. We have to fend for ourselves. God is reduced from omnipotent Father to Big Brother. He is powerful, but not all powerful.

Job never flirts with this solution. Like most people, he implicitly argues that if there is a God at all worthy of the name, he must be omnipotent. If he created the universe, he must be omnipotent, for it takes infinite power to create everything out of nothing. Ordinary language agrees with Job; the adjective we spontaneously affix to the name "God" is *almighty*, as if it is God's first name. Throughout the Bible the question is never whether God is real (only "the fool has said in his heart, 'There is no God' ") or whether God is all powerful (only a pagan polytheist or a modern naturalist would question that) but whether God is good and trustable; what he is up to, and what we are supposed to be up to. Job is a biblical book not only in the sense that it is in the Bible but also in the sense that it assumes the theology of the rest of the Bible. To try to interpret it as contradicting the rest of the Bible, as Kushner and others do—to interpret it as teaching that God is not all powerful or that Job is right and God is wrong or that life is a problem to be solved rationally rather than a mystery to be affirmed by faith (all these notions are essentially Kushner's interpretation)—is to do fundamental violence to the solid foundation of biblical assumptions that neither Job nor the book of Job, neither the character nor the work and its author, ever put into question.

If we cannot solve the "problem of evil" by denying that (1) bad things do happen to good people, as Job's three friends do by saying that Job is not a good person; or by denying that (2) God is all good; or (3) God is all powerful, then the only thing left seems to be (4) denying God's very existence. But this simply magnifies all the terrible consequences of all the other "solutions". Furthermore, it is not Job's or the book of Job's solution, for neither Job nor the author of Job is a "fool". What fifth solution is then possible?

Perhaps the problem cannot be solved at all. Or perhaps it is not a problem but a mystery. Or perhaps there is a solution after all, a partial solution, even on the rational level. Let us look more carefully by considering the argument of Job's three friends. Here it is:

1. Faith premise: God is just.
2. Rational premise: Justice means rewarding the good and punishing the evil.
3. Commonsense premise: Rewards make you happy; punishments make you unhappy.
4. Experiential premise: Job is unhappy.
   Conclusion: Job is evil.

This argument, when unpacked logically, has four different premises from four different sources. The first premise comes from faith, from the nonnegotiable core of Jewish faith in God's *emeth*, God's truth and justice and reliability. It is the faith that God is real, just, good, reliable, and all powerful and rules his world justly. That is the premise Job questions. Everyone who suffers as Job suffered naturally tends to question this premise, whether they successfully resist this temptation or not. We must credit Job's three friends with at least enough faith to resist this temptation. They may malign Job, and that may be as blameworthy as maligning God, but at least they do not malign God. Job flirts with this again and again. He says God invents grievances against him without cause, that if God and Job showed up in court before a neutral judge, Job would win his case—the only reason he is losing is not God's justice but God's power. This is maligning God indeed, indirectly calling him an unjust tyrant. Job (and we) *must* hold on to the first premise, God's justice.

The second premise unpacks the meaning of the key term in the first premise, the term *just*. If God is just, what does that mean? Well, justice means rewarding the good and punishing the evil, not vice versa. It means giving each his due, his "just deserts". This is a premise not from faith but from reason, from rational ethics. It is as basic to ethics as the first premise is to faith. Without a trustable God, there is no religious faith, and without a meaningful justice that discriminates between good and evil and assigns appropriate rewards and punishments, there is no ethics. So far none of the premises seems questionable or modifiable.

The third premise unpacks the predicate of the second, as the second did to the first. If justice means rewards and punishments, in what do rewards and punishments consist? Obviously, many things in the concrete and particular, from money to honor and from execution to fines. But the one thing all rewards have in common is that they give to the person who deserves them something to make him happy, while the one thing all punishments have in common is that they give to the punished person something to make him unhappy. If prisons were spas, they would not be punishments. If money were a disease, it would not be a reward. That is the point of the story of Br'er Rabbit and Br'er Fox, from the Uncle Remus stories. Br'er Fox had tried to catch Br'er Rabbit for years in every conceivable way and never caught him, because Br'er Rabbit was so clever. But one day Br'er Fox caught him. He held him by the ears and said, "Now, Br'er Rabbit, you can choose how you is goin' to die. Do you want to be skinned, roasted, or boiled in oil?" Br'er Rabbit replied,

"You can skin me if you like, and you can roast me if you like, or you can boil me in oil if you like, but please, please, don't throw me in that horrible briar patch!" Br'er Fox saw the gleam of terror in Br'er Rabbit's eye and said, "You know, Br'er Rabbit, that's just exactly what I'm gonna do." And he flung Br'er Rabbit gleefully and hatefully into the briar patch. But instead of pieces of dead rabbit, what Br'er Fox saw in the briar patch was Br'er Rabbit running through the briars laughing, "Fooled you again, Br'er Fox! I was born and bred in a briar patch!" The only reason the story works is the assumption that punishments are supposed to harm you or make you miserable. No one questions this premise. It comes from common sense.

The fourth premise is that Job is unhappy. This premise comes from experience and is even more obvious than the ones before it. Indeed, each of the four premises is more obvious and undeniable than the one before it—which means that only the first, the faith premise, is really in question. No one is tempted to deny the other three premises, but Job is tempted to deny the first. The only other possibility seems to be to draw the logical conclusion, as the three friends do, that Job is miserable because he is suffering deserved punishment, that is, that Job is a great sinner.

But the reader knows this is wrong. God himself said so, to the devil. The reader also knows that it is wrong to deny the first premise. Yet the first premise, God's justice, coupled with three other apparently utterly undeniable premises, logically necessitates the conclusion. What a puzzle!

Let us play a game the book of Job does not play. Let us do some logic. We have translated the existential problem of evil into the logical problem of evil, so we had better solve it on the logical level. (The book, of course, solves it only on the level on which it raises it, the existential level, the lived level. The drama is resolved—how, we shall see later.)

There are three and only three ways to answer any logical argument (as we saw in discussing the argument in Ecclesiastes).

If the terms are not ambiguous, if the premises are not false, and if the process of argumentation is not logically fallacious, then the conclusion has been proved true and there is no way to oppose it except simply to assert your own bullheaded obstinacy, to say, "You proved your point to be true, but I just won't admit it is true." That, of course, says nothing at all about the argument or the conclusion, but it says something about you.

None of the four premises is simply false, and the conclusion logically follows from the premises, but each of the premises contains an ambiguous term. That is how the logical form of the problem of evil can be answered.

The first premise states that God is good and trustable. But the goodness of God cannot mean exactly the same thing as the goodness of man, because God is not man. A good man is not the same as a good dog; for the same reason, the goodness of God is not the same as the goodness of man. The reason is that goodness is proportionate to being. God's being is divine and infinite; man's is finite and human; a dog's is finite and doggy. Each has a goodness proportionate to its nature. For instance, it is not evil for a dog to be sexually promiscuous, as it is for a man. A dog's goodness ("good doggie"), if carried over into a man, would not be goodness but imperfection, regression to merely animal instinct. So it must be with human and divine goodness. The term is analogical, not univocal: its meanings are not wholly or exactly the same but modified, partly the same and partly different. If we were to do, or try to do, some of the things God does, we would not be good but bad. For instance, if a human father deliberately let his child be run over by a car when he could have run into the road to save him, he is not a good father. But God can save us, by miracle, every time we are threatened; yet he does not save us from all harm. Yet he is good in not saving us from all harm, for he sees, in his infinite wisdom, just what sufferings we need for our ultimate fulfillment and wisdom and happiness in the long run, and he sees the spiritual spoiledness that would result from our being saved from every calamity. Human fathers have only a tiny bit of this kind of foresight; that is why it would be wrong for them to play God and let their children suffer, except in a few cases where the human father's knowledge is fairly certain. For instance, it would be wrong for any human father to let his child die because he thought that if the child lived he would not go on to moral and spiritual progress but would regress and eventually die in a worse state. For no earthly father knows such things, as God does. But it would be right for an earthly father to send his child to an unusually difficult school, one that caused the child to sweat at studies and have twice the homework, if the father knew the child was bright and the school was worthwhile. So for us to be good and trustworthy is usually (but not always) for us to save each other from suffering, but this cannot apply to God in the same way. The marching orders for the infantry do not apply to the general, who makes the overall strategy.

This does not mean that God is amoral, or that goodness is simply a creature, not an attribute of the Creator, something God arbitrarily makes and could have made differently, just as he could have made the sky red instead of blue. No, "God is love" and God is also just, but what these moral perfections mean in God exceeds what they mean in us just as goodness in us exceeds goodness in a dog.

The ambiguous term in the second premise is the term *justice*. For us, justice means equality, or at least equal opportunity. It means something almost mathematical. We are all equal before the law. But this is not the deepest meaning of justice. There is a justice in music, a harmony and proportion and relatedness that make for beauty, but it is not equality. It is something much more mysterious, more heavy with meaning, and more wonderful. "By justice the stars are strong", says the poet. The Greeks spoke of a cosmic justice (*dīkē*), "the music of the spheres". This is closer to the divine justice. Is it "just" in the simply mathematical sense that half the human race lacks a womb? Is it just that men have stronger upper body muscles

than women? Is it just, even, that men are superior to monkeys?
(I make an exception for those men who do not think they are
superior to monkeys, as a self-fulfilling prophecy.)

The highest and most mysterious form of divine justice we
have ever heard of is, precisely, the Gospel, the astonishing
events of God's lowering himself to become a man and dying
on a Cross for us. Saint Paul calls this Gospel "the righteousness
of God" in Romans. But this "righteousness", or justice,
centers on the most unjust thing that ever happened in history:
deicide, the murder of the man who least deserved it, the most
innocent, the only innocent, suffering for the guilty. And this
is God's *justice*! Obviously, justice there is something other
than justice here. Here, it is rewarding the good and punishing
the evil. There, it is "all we like sheep have gone astray, we
have turned every one to his own way, and the Lord hath laid
on him the iniquity of us all" (Is 53:6).

In premise three, the ambiguous term is *happy*. Rewards are
in the form of happiness—common sense is right to say that,
of course. But perhaps common sense is not very clear about
what happiness means. We tend to identify it (1) with something immediate and present, not future, long range, or eternal,
and (2) with a conscious subjective feeling of satisfaction of
desire rather than with an objective fact. Perhaps Job is not
happy yet, but he is happy in the end; and perhaps Job does not
feel happy but *is* happy nevertheless.

To see the second point, consider the analogy of health. We
can be healthy without feeling healthy, as when we have a
nagging headache but nothing else is wrong with us. The little
headache takes up the center of our consciousness, and we feel
as if we are going to die, but the objective fact is that we are
very healthy. Our feelings are an imperfect indication of our
health. Alternatively, we may be victims of some dread, fatal
disease and doomed to die in two minutes yet feel perfectly
healthy. Feelings are not an infallible indicator of fact.

Well, what is true on the bodily level can be true on the
spiritual level, too. A Pharisee can feel morally and spiritually

healthy, when in fact he is so rotten that gentle Jesus calls him a tomb full of dead men's bones. A saint can be going through "the dark night of the soul" and feel totally dried up inside, while in fact God is perfecting him like an artist perfecting his masterpiece.

Job may be happy in the sense of being *blessed* without being happy in the sense of being *satisfied*. Job is God's masterpiece, and his sufferings make him even more of a masterpiece. His objective happiness, or perfection, or blessedness (which includes his wisdom and courage and maturity) is in fact attained precisely by means of his subjective unhappiness, or suffering.

Finally, the fourth premise contains the ambiguous term *unhappy*, or *miserable*, which is ambiguous in exactly the way *happy* was ambiguous in the third premise. Job is really blessed in his sufferings, as Christ promised in his Beatitudes: "Blessed are those who mourn . . . blessed are you when men revile you." It makes no sense at all, in the shallow and obvious sense of "happiness", to say, "Happy are you who mourn." But in the deeper, older sense of happiness (blessedness), Job is deeply happy there on his dung heap. He is suffering and not satisfied, but he is blessed and not rejected.

The other ambiguity of the term *happy* also applies to the fourth premise. Job may be short-range unhappy, but he is long-range happy, even in the sense of satisfaction. Job is satisfied at the end (and we will explore why later). He is in a drama, a story, after all, and only in the earlier acts, the earlier chapters. How can you understand the point of Act II until you get to Act V? The problem of evil, as lived rather than as thought, is a problem in a story, in time, and Scripture's one-word answer to the problem is "wait".

When Saint Thomas Aquinas stated in the *Summa* the problem of evil as one of the two objections to the existence of God, he remembered what many philosophers forget: that the solution, God's solution, is concrete, not abstract; dramatic, not schematic; an event in time, not a timeless truth. Saint Thomas, as we saw, stated the problem as follows: " 'God' means infinite goodness. But if one of two contraries is infinite, the other is totally destroyed. Yet evil exists [and is not destroyed]. Therefore God [infinite goodness] does not exist." And he answered it as follows: "As Augustine says, Since God is the highest good, He would not allow any evil to exist in His works unless His omnipotence and goodness were such as to bring good even out of evil." In other words, life, like Job, is like a fairy tale. To get to live happily ever after, you have to go through the dung heap. Evil is only temporary; good is eternal. Once again, in a word, "wait".

But wait in faith. Jesus told Martha, before he raised her brother Lazarus from the dead, "Did I not tell you that if you believe you will see the glory of God?" Seeing is not believing, but believing is seeing, eventually. Job does not wait patiently, but he waits. Job's faith is not sunny and serene, but it is faith. It is not without doubts. (Indeed, his doubts came from his faith. When faith is full, it is open and can include doubts; when it is weak, it cannot tolerate doubts.) But Job remains a hero of faith. He waits in faith, and he sees the glory of God. He is blessed in the very waiting, in the dung, in the agony; and he is doubly blessed in the finding, in the end.

2. The Problem of Faith versus Experience

So far, we have only scratched the surface. The problem of evil is only the most obvious problem in Job, the one all the books talk about. But deeper than this there are other levels, like underground caves or even cities, whole realms of mystery and meaning less amenable to clear analysis and simple solution. A second level of problem is the conflict not between faith and reason, as in the problem of evil, but between faith and experience, Job's faith and his experience. Here we have not a philosophical puzzle but a child's tears. Throughout Scripture and throughout Job's life, God approaches with a "sales pitch": "Trust me." God's *emeth*, or fidelity, is here not a datum in a logical puzzle but a lifeline, and the rope seems to have broken. Throughout the Bible the promise is always that fidelity to God will be rewarded by God's fidelity to you and to his promises of reward. The righteous prosper; the wicked perish. So Job buys into this advertisement, this faith. He stakes his whole life on righteousness, obedience, fidelity, piety—and what is his reward? Loss of his possessions, his children, his wife's loyalty, his friends' respect, his health, and even, it seems, his identity and his God (as we shall see in two subsequent, even deeper levels). Worst of all is God's abandonment, Job's "my God, my God, why hast thou forsaken me?" experience. "I cried out, and the Lord heard me and answered me from his holy mountain"—this is the constant theme of the Psalms. But Job's experience seems to falsify it. God may be there, but he is not there for Job.

Here is what Job's experience seems to teach him about God. God seems like the father in the following cruel joke. A father said to his little son, "Son, I want to teach you one of life's most important lessons: how to trust your father. Get up on that five-foot-high wall and jump into my arms. I'll catch you." "But Daddy, I'm afraid. Don't make me climb up there." "I know you're afraid, son. But I want you to do this for me." "All right, Daddy. Here I come. . . . Whee! You caught me!" "Of course I caught you. I promised, didn't I?" "Can we go home now?" "No, I want you to jump from that ten-foot-high wall now." "Ooh, Daddy, I'm scared." "Trust me." "OK. Here I come. . . . Whee! You caught me again!" "Of course I did." "Can we go home now?" "After just one more time. This time, jump from that twenty-foot-high wall." "Ooh, Daddy, I'm so scared." "Trust me." "OK. Here I come . . . " And the father stepped back at the last minute and let the boy slam against the sidewalk. From a pool of blood and tears came the question, "Daddy, Daddy, why did you do that?" The answer: "To teach you life's most important lesson, Son: Never trust anybody, not even your father."

It is a bad joke, and a cruel joke, but that is what life looks like to Job. He had trusted God, and now God stepped back and let him down with a crash. Job's faith says that if you trust God, you will be rewarded. Job's experience says the opposite. Job must have been a remarkable man of faith to have held on to his faith (though just barely) in the teeth of such apparently conclusive refutation from experience.

Job is traditionally regarded as a hero of faith. This shows that faith, for an Old Testament Jew (and also for a New Testament Christian) is more fundamental than the old Baltimore Catechism's definition of it (though that in turn is much deeper than most modern textbooks describe it): "An act of the intellect, prompted by the will, by which we believe what God has revealed on the authority of the One who revealed it". Faith for Job is not primarily an act of the intellect but of the guts or the heart. Faith here is *emeth*, fidelity, trustability, promise keeping, reliability. Job is a culture hero, for he tests the fundamental value of his culture, *emeth*, in his life as in a test tube. He stakes his life on it; indeed, he gives up much of his life for it. But the ironic question is: Who is testing whom? It seems to Job as if Job's experience is testing God's fidelity, but in fact, as the reader knows from that peep behind the scenes in chapter 1, it is God who is testing Job's fidelity.

The test is only secondarily the loss of all Job's earthly goods. The test is fundamentally Job's apparent loss of God. Proof of this is the fact that even before Job gets any of his earthly goods back, he is satisfied at the end just because he got God back. But for thirty-seven agonizing chapters, he does not find God, though he seeks him. His faith tells him, in effect, "Seek and you shall find; all who seek, find." But his experience tells him the opposite. No one seeks as much, as passionately, as needily as Job seeks; yet he finds nothing. "I go to the east, and he is not there. I turn to the west and he is not there either" (Job 23:8–9). Why? Why does God not answer Job? How is the God of faith, the faithful one, compatible with the experience of seeking without finding?

The experience is not confined to Job. As C. S. Lewis put it, in *A Grief Observed*, reflecting on the lack of consolation his faith gave him after the death of his wife:

> Meanwhile, where is God? This is one of the most disquieting symptoms. When you are happy, so happy that you have no sense of needing Him, so happy that you are tempted to feel His claims upon you as an interruption, if you remember yourself and turn to Him with gratitude and praise, you will be—or so it feels—welcomed with open arms. But go to Him when your need is desperate, when all other help is vain, and what do you find? A door slammed in your face, and a sound of bolting and double bolting on the inside. After that, silence.

In previous ages, especially the Middle Ages, which were strong on reason but weak on psychological introspection, and attention to feeling and experience, the crucial problem was the relation between faith and reason. (Some of the philosophical and scientific conclusions of Aristotle seemed to contradict the Christian Faith.) In our age, which is weak on reason (and even doubts reason's power to discover or prove objective truth) and strong on psychology and experience, the crucial problem is the relation between faith and experience. Today many more people lose their faith because they experience suffering and think God has let them down than lose their faith because of any rational argument. Job is a man for all seasons but especially for ours. His problem is precisely our problem.

What is the solution? Specifically, why does Job experience God's absence when God promised to be present? One part of the answer is easy: God is testing Job's faith. Job must believe in God as real and present and faithful not only because it is easy to believe, because things are going well, because experience so confirms faith that faith is almost unnecessary; he must also learn to believe in God out of sheer faith, even when experience and appearances seem to contradict faith—like Jesus on the Cross, forsaken by God, without consolation of any kind. Such faith is infinitely more precious than the cheap and dispensable faith that leads you in the same direction as experience does. Teeth-gritting faith is valuable not because suffering is valuable in itself or because teeth gritting is valuable in itself but because such faith comes from the deep, eternal center of the person, the I, the will, not from feelings, not from the parts of the person that are dependent on the environment and what happens in the world. For the world will pass away, but the self will not. What the self decides in time is ratified in eternity. The stronger the choice for God at this obscure and unemotional center of the self, the surer and deeper will be the eternal salvation of the whole self. The will is the custodian of the feelings and must learn to lead them, not follow them.

That is the obvious and easy part of the answer. God is toughening and perfecting Job's faith, Job's fidelity, in the furnace of suffering. But there is another part of the answer, which comes not from the nature of Job but from the nature of God. Because of what God is, he cannot show up in answer to Job's questions, in function of Job's needs. God will not answer Job because God is not the Answer Man. He is not the Answerer, the Responder. He is the Initiator, the Questioner. He is not second but first, "in the beginning". His name (which reveals his essence) is "I AM", not "HE IS". God exists in the First Person Singular. He is Subject, not Object, not even object of Job's searchings and questionings.

Everyone who has ever met God as distinct from a concept of God, all the saints and mystics, everyone, in other words, who is like Job rather than like Job's three theologian friends, has said the same thing: when you meet God, you cannot put the meeting into words, much less the God you meet. God cannot be an object of our concepts. Concepts shatter like broken eyeglasses, like broken eyes—in fact, like broken I's. No longer am I I and God my Thou, my object; now God is I, and I am his thou, his object. Thus the mystics say such strange things about the self, as if it were an illusion or destroyed in this encounter. The illusion that is destroyed is not the self itself but its usual standpoint in which I am I, the center, and God appears on my screen somewhere. *This* self is illusion, and God shatters it by reversing the standpoint: we appear on his screen. We are his object, not he ours.

That is why Jesus manifests his divinity so powerfully by always reversing the relationship into which questioners try to put him. His enemies try to pin him down; he pins them down. They try to classify him; he classifies them. They try to judge him; he judges them. Even his friends try to unveil him, understand him, reveal him, get the mystery of who he is to come out of hiding; but every encounter accomplishes the opposite: *they* are unveiled, understood, revealed; the mystery of who *they* are has to come out of hiding when in the presence of the divine Light. "Shall we stone the adulteress or not?"—"Let him without sin cast the first stone." "Should we pay taxes to Caesar or not?"—"Give God what is God's and Caesar what is Caesar's." (They were robbing both.) "Who is my neighbor?"—"Go and be a neighbor, like the good Samaritan." Whenever you try to test him, he tests you, for he is the teacher and you are the student, not vice versa.

Viktor Frankl speaks of this experience of startling, sudden reversal of standpoint or perspective in the context of the concentration camps. He says in *Man's Search for Meaning* that many of the prisoners learned to stop asking the question "What is the meaning of life?" and realized that life was asking them what *their* meaning was. Instead of continuing to ask "Life, why are you doing this to me? I demand an answer!" they realized that life was questioning them and demanding an answer—an answer in deeds, not just words. They had to respond to this question, this challenge, by being responsible. Even when they did not interpret life as God's instrument, even when "life" was an abstraction rather than a person, they felt it questioning them, as the millions of people who have had near-death experiences felt the "Being of Light" questioning them, rather than vice versa. For the one thing you cannot light up is light. Light is the best physical symbol for God because it is the only physical thing that cannot be an object of sight. God cannot be an object of sight, physical or mental. Saint Thomas Aquinas says that we know God correctly only when we know him as unknowable. Scripture says the same thing: "No man has seen God at any time; only the only-begotten Son, in the bosom of the Father, has made him known" (Jn 1:18). If God had not taken the initiative to reveal himself, there is no way we could know him. When we want to know a stone, it is all passive, and we are all active. When we want to know an animal, it is a little bit active, and it can run away and hide. When we want to know another person, we are dependent on the other's free choice to be known, as well as our own free choice to know: the two roles are equal. Finally, when we want to know God, all the activity must begin from his side.

So God cannot show up in answer to Job's questions as if he were a library book (which is the way Job's three friends treat God). Job pushes buttons, but the God machine does not work, not because it is broken but because it is not a machine. Job finally realizes this when God shows up in his true character as Questioner, not as Answerer. That is why Job repents in the end (Job 42:6). What he repents of is not some specific sin he has committed and hidden, as the three friends suspect, but of his metaphysical mistake, his sin against the grammar of being, his playing the part of God. The best words Job uttered were his last: "The words of Job are ended." Only when Job shuts up does God show up.

Most of us talk too much. It is amazing how short Jesus' sayings are. When we pray, who does most of the talking? Is it the most important party to the conversation or the least important one? If we had the opportunity to converse with some great person, like Mother Teresa or Alexandr Solzhenitsyn, would we want to do most of the talking, or would we want to listen most of the time? Why do we talk so much to God that we have no time to listen? How patient God must be, waiting until we get rid of all our mental and verbal noise and hoping that we do not then immediately turn from addressing him to addressing the world. In that split second of silence between the time we stop talking to God and start talking to the world, God gets more graces into us than at any other time outside the sacraments.

Job says at one point to his three talkative friends, "What a plague your need to have the last word is!" They are like soap opera queens, always waiting at the exit door to deliver the "zinger" and then leaving. But Job does to God exactly what Job's friends do to Job! They do not listen to Job because they are too busy talking to him, and Job does not listen to God because he is too busy talking to him. What Job repents of in the end, when God appears, is not that he was worse than his three friends but that he was just like them! They were like the four Zen monks who made a vow of lifelong silence. One day, one of them let out a single word. The second said to him, "You broke your vow of silence." The third said to the second, "You're a bigger fool than he is. You did, too!" The fourth smiled to himself and said, "I'm the only one who didn't."

Have you ever kept silent for half an hour, speaking with neither your lips nor your mind? You are going to have to learn that art if you want to endure Heaven, because there will be silence in Heaven for half an hour after the opening of the seventh seal (Rev 8:1).

Only in silence do faith and experience perfectly line up, for faith tells us that God is I AM, and silence lets us experience his I-ness as well as his am-ness, his priority as well as his reality. All talk subtly falsifies God. As Lao-tzu put it, "Those that say don't know; those that know don't say." For "the Way that can be spoken of is not the eternal Way". Nevertheless, the Way has spoken to us. "In the beginning was the Word", not just the silence. We need silence not because God is silence but because God is Word. Only in silence do faith and experience totally line up.

3. The Problem of the Meaning of Life

The greatest of all questions, the question that includes all other questions, is the one Job asks God in Job 10:18: "Why did you bring me out of the womb?" In other words, what kind of a story am I in? What are my lines? What play is this? Why was I born? Why am I living? What's it all about, Alfie? It is Ecclesiastes' question, too, but Job gets an answer, while Ecclesiastes does not. Pascal calls them the two greatest philosophers, and I agree. But why did Job get an answer and Ecclesiastes not? For the same reason Moses got an answer to the questions about which philosophers had speculated endlessly and fruitlessly for ages: Who is God? What is his name? What is his nature? Moses had the good sense to ask him! (See Ex 3:14.) Ecclesiastes is like Job's three friends: endlessly philosophizing *about* God. Job is like Moses: Job asks *God*; he seeks God's face. And "all who seek, find".

But not for a long time. Why the delay? What is the meaning of the delay? Job's life, about which he asks, is twofold: seeking and finding. Clearly, the answer to the question: What is the meaning, purpose, end, point, and consummation of life? is in finding God. But what about the other half, the seeking? For whom does God let Job suffer and seek and agonize? What did God have to prove? Is Job a bug in a test tube to satisfy God's idle or sadistic curiosity? Or did God turn up the heat under the test tube just to win his bet with the devil?

Clearly, God does nothing for Satan's sake, for evil's sake. There is no justification for Good kowtowing to evil, and no need for omnipotence to make the smallest compromise to evil. And clearly not for God's sake, for omniscience has no need of experiments. God did not need to know Job's faith would hold. But Job did. All the agony and waiting must have been for Job's sake, for Job's good, for Job's beatitude. Even the cross "is the gift God gives to his friends", says one of the saints. Especially the cross.

This world is "a vale of soul making", a great sculptor's shop, and we are the statues. To be finished, the statues must endure many blows of the chisel and be hardened in the fire. This is not optional. Once we lost our original innocence, the way back to God *has* to be painful, for the Old Man of sin will keep on complaining and paining at each step toward his enemy, goodness. Saying "not my will but thine be done" was ecstatic joy in Eden and will be in Heaven, but it is life's most difficult (and most necessary) task now. Without it, we have no face with which to face God. Why could Job see God face to face and live? Because Job got a face through his suffering faith. As C. S. Lewis says at the end of his novel *Till We Have Faces*, "How can we meet the gods face to face till we have faces?"

That is the meaning of life: getting a face, becoming real, becoming yourself—but in ways and toward an end not even dreamed of by the pop psychologists who say these things so casually. Yes, life is a process of becoming yourself—but this is done by suffering, not by sinning; by saying No as well as saying Yes; by climbing against the gravity of the selfish self, not by the direct paths of "self-realization" and "self-actualization". The meaning of life is war. And our enemies are not less but more real and formidable than flesh and blood. Unless we defeat them, we will die a death infinitely more hopeless and horrible than any battlefield gore. It is not easy to get a face. Job is no exception, but the rule; the trouble God had to bring him through is ours, too, in one way or another. However, Job's way is unusually visible, extraordinarily externalized. Not all of us lose our children, our health, our possessions, and our confidence in one day. But all of us must learn to lose everything but God, for all of us will die, and you cannot take anything with you but God.

Philosophers give some noble and beautiful answers to the question of life's meaning, purpose, and end: virtue, wisdom, honor, character, joy, freedom, "the true, the good, and the beautiful"—but they ignore the grubby little question that nags us as we admire these true ideals: How? How is this dwarf to fly like that eagle? How can I get from here to there, from Before to After, from cretin to Christ? "All right, now you know what you are made for: to become a shining, radiant, strong, noble creature that can endure the perfect light of Heaven, a veritable god or goddess. So get on with it, please. Turn into one. Be ye holy as the Lord your God is holy. Be ye perfect as your Father in Heaven is perfect." Right! You see, a bit of doing is necessary. A bit of sculpting. A bit of spiritual warfare. What is remarkable is not that God hits us with so many blows of the sculptor's chisel but that he manages with so few. What is remarkable, once you see the distance between where you are now and where you are destined to be, is how God's mercy succeeds in bringing us there with so little trouble, so little pain. What is remarkable is not how many bad things happen to good people but how many good things happen to bad people. And this is what Job realizes as soon as he sees God at the end, and this is why he is answered and satisfied. And we will be, too.

God could have created us in Heaven to begin with, happy and sinless. Why did he instead give us a time of testing on earth? For the same reason a good teacher does not give the student all the answers. We appreciate the truth more when we find it for ourselves. Then it is more truly ours. The truth here is not just objective truth but our own identity, our own true face. God designed it, but God arranges for us to cosculpt it, to cocreate our own very selves by our choices and experiences in time. We find out who we are only by living.

This means that until we are finished, we do not really know who we are (once we stop fooling ourselves). It means that every life is a prolonged identity crisis. Job's is only more visible and sudden. Once he was Job the righteous, Job the just, Job the good example, Job, God's favorite. Now all these labels are torn away, and he is a heap of sores on a dung heap scratching himself with a potsherd. No wonder his three friends, when they arrive, do not recognize him (Job 2:12)!

The Jerusalem Bible's apt footnote reminds the reader of the suffering servant of God in Isaiah 52 and 53, who was the outcast, like a leper, one from whom men hide their faces, one who was taken outside the city gates to be crucified, outside humanity, excommunicated from his people, "a worm and no man", as Psalm 22 says that he recited from the cross. Job is a Christ figure, so starkly unrecognizable that he is starkly recognizable, for this is part of what Christ is: unrecognizable, "a worm, and no man . . . outcast of the people".

The only place Job can find his identity is in his Author and Designer. The same is true of everyone, for we are all characters invented by one Author, and how could the character find his identity outside the Author? Thus, Job finds his identity only in finding his God; Job solves problem three (his identity and purpose) only in solving problem four, the deepest problem of all, the God problem, to which we must now turn.

4. The Problem of God

The problem of God in Job is not whether God exists. Only the fool says in his heart that there is no God, and he says it not because reason and evidence tell him but because his deceptive, wish-fulfillment desires tell him to pretend there is no God so that he can sin without punishment. (That is the psychoanalysis of both the psalmist [Ps 14] and the apostle [Rom 1:18–2:1]).

Nor is the problem of God who or what God is in himself. That is the problem of the theologian or the philosopher. Job's problem is: What (or rather who) is God to me? What is the relationship?

There are two problems of God in Job: the first concerns Job and the search; the second concerns God and the finding. The first problem is why Job is in a right God-relationship in his searching. The second is why God, once found, proves totally adequate to answer all of Job's questions and agonies even without answering any of Job's questions and even before he gives Job back all the worldly goods he took away. There are two puzzling sections in Job that pinpoint these two problems. The first is Job 42:7, where God approves Job's heretical and blasphemous words and disapproves the orthodox and pious words of the three friends. The second is Job 42:1–6, where Job, the most demanding and impatient and hard-to-satisfy man in the Bible, is totally satisfied.

The first puzzling phrase reads as follows: "When Yahweh had said all this to Job, he turned to Eliphaz of Teman. 'I burn with anger against you and your two friends', he said 'for not speaking truthfully about me as my servant Job has done.' " (Job 42:7). But Job, by his own admission, uttered "wild words" (Job 6:2–3). He thought God was his enemy, thought God was inventing grievances against him without cause, and even thought God would lose a fair court case against him! How awful that would be: to win in court against God. What hope would there be then? Our only hope, as Kierkegaard so arrestingly puts it in a sermon title, is "On the Edification Implied in the Thought That Over Against God We Are Always in the Wrong". If the source of all right is himself wrong, then there is no right reality for us to be reconciled with, to hope in, to find our way back home to. Job's words are foolish, wild, even blasphemous. How can God say he spoke truthfully?

And how can God say the three friends did not speak the truth? Every single thing they say can be found in dozens of passages elsewhere in the Bible. They defend God; they are pious; they are orthodox. Their viewpoint is simply "let God be true and every man a liar" (Rom 3:4). Their desire is simply "arise, O God, let not man prevail" (Ps 9:19). How can this be false and Job true?

One "solution" taken by radical interpreters is that Job was written by a heretic and contradicts the rest of the Bible. (Everyone who says that really seems to mean that the rest of the Bible is heretical because it contradicts Job.) The theory is that Job is really right and God really wrong, Job the hero and God the villain. This is the same folly, of course, that Job dallies with in imagining his winning his suit against God in court. There has to be a better way.

There is. Notice carefully what God says in Job 42:7—not that Job spoke truth but that he spoke truthfully, and not that the three friends did not speak truth but that they did not speak truthfully, as Job did. What is the difference between speaking truth and speaking truthfully?

It is the difference between a noun and an adverb, between truth in the content of what is spoken and truth in the act of speaking itself. Whether or not you speak the truth is an objective question, whereas whether or not you speak truthfully is a subjective question, a personal question. Job did not always speak the truth, but he always spoke truthfully. His words were not always in the truth, but he was. He had the quality of truth, *emeth*, fidelity, in his being and his acting. He had what Kierkegaard called (somewhat misleadingly) "truth as subjectivity" (in *Concluding Unscientific Postscript*).

What does this mean specifically? Job sticks to God, retains intimacy, passion, and care, while the three friends are satisfied with correctness of words, "dead orthodoxy". Job's words do not accurately reflect God, as the three friends' words do, but Job himself is in a true relationship to God, as the three friends are not: a relationship of heart and soul, life-or-death passion. No one can be truly related to God without life-or-death passion. To be related to God in a way that is only finite, partial, held back, or calculating is not truly to be related to God. God is everything or nothing. Job thinks God has let him down, so that in a sense God has become nothing to him. That is a mistake, but Job at least knows it must be all or nothing. God is infinite love, and the opposite of love is not hate but indifference. Job's love for God is infected with hate, but the three friends' love for God is infected with indifference. Job stays married to God and throws dishes at him; the three friends have a polite nonmarriage, with separate bedrooms and separate vacations. The family that fights together stays together.

There is a second reason why Job spoke truthfully about God. The most obvious and important difference between the speeches of Job and the speeches of the three friends is one that escapes our notice for the same reason the capital letters naming the continents escape our notice on maps, and Poe's "purloined letter" (in the famous short story by that name), exposed to plain view, escaped the notice of the police who were carefully searching every nook and cranny for it: it is too big, too close up, too obvious, like the nose on your face (mine, anyway). It took Martin Buber to point it out to me, and this one discovery suddenly lit up the whole book of Job as no other could: the difference is simply that the three friends speak *about* God while Job speaks *to* God.

This is speaking "truthfully" because it is speaking to God as God is, that is, as always present Person, not as absent object. Speaking to God in the second person is one person closer to the first person singular that I AM is in his own essential being than speaking about him in the third person. Buber says, "God is the Thou who can never become an It." He also says, "God can only be addressed, not expressed", for the same reason.

Suppose I am in your presence, and you start talking to a third party about me, ignoring me. Not only is this highly insulting; it is also metaphysically inaccurate. It treats the real as the unreal; it treats presence as if it were absence. And that is what the three friends always do. They never pray, only preach. Job is always praying, like Augustine in the *Confessions*: every word is uttered either to God or in his presence. That is why there is such blinding light even amid the confusion: Job insists on standing in the presence of God, who is light. The three friends try to generate their own light by reasoning about God as a proper concept. God is right there all the time, between Job and the friends, so to speak, as the fifth party around the dung heap. Job believes this fundamental truth and therefore speaks truthfully (that is, to the God who really is present), while the three friends act as if God were absent. For the second person ("you") means presence, while the third person ("he") means absence.

The most practical lesson we can learn from Job—the most practical lesson we can ever learn from anything—is "the practice of the presence of God", the simplest and most fundamental exercise in realism and in sanctity. The two are identical, for both mean simply living in reality, not illusion, acting as if what is real is real. And the most fundamental reality is the God who is present.

The other puzzling passage is Job's reply to God's speech:

This was the answer Job gave to Yahweh:

I know that you are all-powerful:
What you conceive, you can perform.
I am the man who obscured your designs
with my empty-headed words.
I have been holding forth on matters I cannot understand,
on marvels beyond me and my knowledge. . . .
I knew you then only by hearsay,
But now, having seen you with my own eyes,
I retract all I have said,
and in dust and ashes I repent (Job 42:1–6).

Job is the most demanding man in the Bible, the "doubting Thomas" of the Old Testament. Why is this Jewish Socrates suddenly satisfied? God did not answer any of his questions. Instead, all he seemed to say was "What do you know, anyway? What right do you have to think you can know the answer, anyway? Who do you think you are, anyway?" Even an ordinary man would be disappointed at such an answer; how much more disappointed should this arch-questioner be?

Let us conduct a little thought experiment to find out why Job was satisfied. Suppose that God had given Job what Job expected instead of what Job got. Suppose that God answered every one of Job's questions with total clarity and total adequacy. (God could certainly do that if he wanted.) Suppose God wrote the world's definitive theology book for Job. Now, what do you think would have been the result?

I think I know, because I think I know Job. Job would have been satisfied for about five seconds after he finished the book, or perhaps even five minutes. But then more questions would have arisen, like the Hydra's heads: questions about questions, questions about answers, questions about interpretations of God's answers. Every answer produces ten more questions to a mind like Job's, that is, the mind of a first-rate, honest, and passionate philosopher. Then the intellectual warfare would have started again. The hundreds of little soldiers coming out of Job's head would have to be met by a hundred big warriors coming out of God. And, of course, they would be met. But then there would be another hundred, or a thousand. The human mind has an infinite capacity to wonder. Nothing can stop it, not even answers, for each answer elicits ten more questions. Eventually we would have an intellectual battlefield strewn to capacity with the corpses of slain ideas, refuted misunderstandings, a mile high. They would accumulate exponentially, and they would stand between Job and God, as they stood between Job's three friends and God. The danger of truth is that it gets obscured by truths. There is only one way to overcome that danger, and God took that way with Job. The way consists of two parts. The first part is negative: not to tell the whole truth in words, not to give answers, even true and adequate answers, not to cut off one of the Hydra's heads lest it sprout two new ones. Thus, God does not answer Job's question; God answers Job instead, and that is the second part, the heart part. Just as Jesus constantly answers the questioner instead of the question, since he sees that the real question is the questioner, not the question, the heart and not the words, so here God answers Job's deepest heart quest: to see God face to face; to see Truth, not truths; to *meet* Truth, not just to know it. Job is satisfied with the only answer that could possibly have satisfied him, in time or in eternity, the only answer that can satisfy us in time or in eternity, the only answer that can overcome boredom and eventual "vanity of vanities", the definitive answer to Ecclesiastes, as to the three friends: the Answerer, not the answer.

"I had heard of you with the hearing of the ear; but now my eye sees you." This is the climax to Job. This is the most important verse in the book. This explains everything that happened, why God brought Job through the whole dung heap: to this end. This is the end of life, the meaning of life, the purpose of life. This is the solution to the problem of evil, and the solution to the problem of the conflict between faith and experience, and the solution to the problem of the meaning of life, and the solution to the problem of my identity, and the solution to the problem of God, of who God is for me. This is the answer to everything. No one, not even Job, can ever be dissatisfied with this answer. No one will have any more questions once he sees this answer. No one will ever feel let down, cheated, or disappointed with this answer, no matter how demanding and dissatisfied he is with everything else. This is the answer that fills the infinite, God-shaped vacuum that is the human heart. This is God.

The greatest question ever asked and the greatest answer ever given, in my opinion, are in an incident near the end of the life of Saint Thomas Aquinas. Thomas was alone in the chapel, he thought (but his friend Reginald was watching and swore under oath that he saw and heard these events), and praying before the altar. A voice came from the mouth of Christ on the crucifix: "You have written well of me, Thomas. What will you have as a reward?" It was the same question with which Jesus began his public ministry, in John's Gospel, the great question: "What do you want?" (Jn 1:38). And the equally great answer Thomas gave to God, the answer that puts a lump in my throat and a bird in my heart every time I say it, was, "Only yourself, Lord". The theologian who found thousands of answers—more answers, and more adequate answers, than any other theologian in history—wants only one thing, "the one thing needful" that Mary wanted and Jesus wanted Martha to want (Lk 10:42): himself. That is why even Job was satisfied. He did not get what he thought he wanted, but he got what he really wanted. He did not get what his head and his consciousness thought they wanted, but he got what his heart and his deep unconscious knew they wanted, the thing we all want. We cannot help it: God made us that way. Only one key fits that lock; only one Romeo satisfies that Juliet. "Deep calls unto deep"—only infinity can marry infinity. Just as no animal was adequate for Adam (Gen 2:18–24), no creature is adequate for the human heart, and *a fortiori* no concept. Concepts are pictures, and men cannot marry pictures (though many of us try and relate more to the picture we have in our mind of what we dream our spouse or friend should be than to the real other who bursts the bounds of all pictures). Job is satisfied because all life is courtship, and now he finally gets married. The Beatific Vision that awaits all believers in Heaven is granted to Job for a moment on earth.

It is the difference between secondhand knowledge and firsthand knowledge, between "the hearing of the ear" and "the seeing of the eye". Job had heard about God, but now he sees God. It is as if you had never met your father because he was away in the French Foreign Legion, and he sent letters to you that were transmitted and interpreted to you by your mother (Mother Church), and then one day he stepped through the door and said, "Here I am". Suppose the letters were perfectly accurate and adequate and interpreted perfectly by your mother. The difference would still be infinite between "the hearing of the ear" and "the seeing of the eye". One moment of his presence would be worth infinitely more than all the letters in the world.

Saint Augustine, in his sermon "On the Pure Love of God", imagines God coming to you with a question similar to the one he asked Saint Thomas. The point is a kind of self-test to find out whether you have "the pure love of God", that is, whether you are obeying the first and greatest commandment, to love God with your whole heart and soul, in that deep, obscure center of your being where your "fundamental option" decides your eternal destiny. Augustine supposes that God proposed to you a deal and said, "I will give you anything you want. You can possess the whole world. Nothing will be impossible for you. You will have infinite power. Nothing will be a sin, nothing forbidden. You will never die, never have pain, never have anything you do not want and always have anything you do want—except for just one thing: you will never see my face." Would you take that deal? If not, you have the pure love of God. For look what you just did: you gave up the world, and more—all possible worlds, all imagined worlds, all desired worlds—just for God. Augustine asks, "Did a chill arise in your heart when you heard the words 'you will never see my face'?" That chill is the most precious thing in you; that is the pure love of God.

Job felt that chill throughout his sufferings. The thing he keeps talking about is not his sores or his lost possessions or even his lost family but rather his lost God. Apparently he was Godforsaken; apparently he would never see God's face. That is the thing he longed for most, even if it meant death. He said in effect what Augustine said in the *Confessions*: "Let me die, only let me see Thy face, lest I die with longing to see it." (Or, in another translation, "Let me die, lest I die; only let me see Thy face.")

Only one thing in life is guaranteed: not happiness, not the pursuit of happiness, not liberty, not even life. The only thing we are absolutely guaranteed is the only thing we absolutely need: God. And wisdom consists essentially in absolutely wanting that which we absolutely need, in conforming our wants to reality. Job is incomparably wiser than Ecclesiastes because of that. We must identify with Job, not Ecclesiastes, for Ecclesiastes' vanity is the philosophy of Hell, while Job's search is the philosophy of Purgatory, and everyone graduates from the University of Purgatory with honors into Heaven.

SONG OF SONGS:

Life as Love

Before I write anything about Song of Songs, I must confess and confront a problem: I am way over my head, out of my depth, playing Little League baseball in a major league park. This book has been the favorite of the greatest saints and mystics, such as Saint Bernard of Clairvaux, Saint John of the Cross, and Saint Thomas Aquinas, who was writing a commentary on it when he died. (How fitting—God cut short the wedding photographer's work when the honeymoon suite was ready.) How can I play in their park?

I cannot, of course. I simply have no solution to the problem. So let us rush in anyway where angels fear to tread. Let us be fools together. We may not be able to play in their league, but we can play the same game. Song of Songs is about love, of course, and love is for everyone.

Another problem at the beginning: this is the only book in the Bible (except for the shorter version of Esther) that never once mentions God.[1] How can this book be the saints' favorite?

That question is much easier to answer: because God is everywhere in this book, symbolically. The bridegroom, Solomon, the Solar King, is a symbol for God, and his chosen bride a symbol for the soul, or the chosen people, Israel, or the Church, the new Israel. Symbolically interpreted, this book is the most intimate book in the Bible. It describes the ultimate purpose of life, which we found at the end of Job: the meeting and marriage between ourselves and God. This is the highest and holiest and happiest hope of the human heart, the thing we were all born hungering for, hunting for, longing for. This is the last chapter of life's story, the point and purpose of it all.

It is also the hidden key to the rest of the Bible. The Bible is about real life, of course—it is the most realistic book ever written. And the point of the real story of life is love. The whole Bible is a love story because God, the author, is love. Behind the appearances of a war story, a detective story, a

[1] Due to an ambiguity in the original Hebrew, translations of Song 8:6 differ. In some translations, such as the Jerusalem Bible, the word *Yahweh* is used.

tragedy, a comedy, or a farce, life is a love story. Thus Song of Songs is the definitive answer to the question of Ecclesiastes and to the quest of Job.

It is a double love story, vertical and horizontal, divine and human. The two great commandments are to love God and to love neighbor. Thus this love poem is to be interpreted on two levels, divine and human. The bridegroom symbolizes God, but he is also any man, literally; and the bride symbolizes the soul, but she is also every woman, literally. To interpret a book or a passage symbolically is not to abandon the literal interpretation. There is a ridiculous, indefensible prejudice among most Bible scholars, both professional and amateur, that we must choose between the symbolic and the literal interpretations of any given book or passage. Fundamentalists automatically bristle at the very word *symbolic*, and modernists automatically bristle at the word *literal*. I think it is high time we rediscovered the riches of the eminently sage and sane "fourfold method of exegesis" of Saint Thomas and the medievals and recapture the hermeneutical heights from which we have fallen.

Song of Songs uses romantic love and marriage rather than any one of the many other human forms of love as its chosen symbol for the love of God because romantic love and marriage comprise the fullest and completest of all human loves. One of the things we shall see in our exploration of the text (point number 24) is just that: the inclusion of friendship, affection, desire, and charity in a rich blend, like a gourmet coffee.

Husband and wife give to each other as much as it is humanly possible to give: their whole selves, body and soul, life, time, friends, world, possessions, children—nothing is to be held back. That is why the Church opposes artificial contraception: because it is the deliberate holding back of the procreative ingredient in marriage, just as test tube babies are the deliberate holding back of the unitive ingredient, and Victorian, puritanical fears hold back the joyful erotic ingredient. God designed all three to be one: unitive, procreative, and erotic, "two in one flesh" intimacy, third-party procreation, and first-party self-forgetful ecstasy. It is all here. This is the next step from Job, the step from Purgatory to Heaven. Ecclesiastes' vanity was Hell on earth, Job's suffering was Purgatory on earth, and Solomon's love is Heaven on earth. Earth is a foretaste, or a foreplay. When death opens earth's exit doors, and the edible light of God's love streams over the astonished, longing eyes of the purified penitent in showers of gold, he is at that moment in Heaven even if he is also in Purgatory. The very washrooms of Heaven's mansion are of gold; the very purgatorial showers that wash away sin's last stains are the showers of God's love. That is why the saints say there are both suffering and joy in Purgatory. Though the scabs tear and the dirt tries to cling against the golden onrush, we will not cringe in Purgatory's shower but with upturned face will ask for more. That is exactly the position of Job when God comes to him. Though his feet are still on his dung heap, his head is in the glory.

This is a parable of the position of every Christian. For Christ did not establish an immediate Heaven on earth. He did not set right all the ills of the world by his first coming; he only planted the seed of that universal redemption. The field of earth and of our human nature is now no longer barren but full of the seed of divine life. But it takes time for the seed to grow, for the Kingdom to come, and we are commanded to pray and work for that coming, that growth, even if we do not yet see the fruits, or even the blossoms, or even the leaves, or even the green growth visible above the ground of the supernatural plant God planted in the world by the Incarnation and in our souls by faith and baptism and the new birth.

Song of Songs completes our *Divine Comedy*, but we must thank Ecclesiastes and Job, too, for it was Job who brought us here, and it was Ecclesiastes who moved us to seek this "here", this Heaven, through honesty about the awfulness of the alternative.

Upon first reading Song of Songs, many modern readers are

puzzled that anyone, much less most of the human race for centuries, would claim that this is the greatest of all love poems. Evidently there is more here than meets the unaided eye. If the eye is aided with the binocular vision of a lover's lens and a poet's lens, dimensions and depths can be seen that are startlingly beautiful. Here are a few of them—twenty-six characteristics of love, both human and divine, that the poem implies. For more, both in quantity and quality, go to the saints.

1. Love Is a Song

The first and most obvious thing Song of Songs says about love it says in its very title: that love is a song. Now this is an image or symbol, of course. Love is not a literal, physical song, though it naturally expresses itself in that form. What is suggested by this image?

God is love, and music is the language of love; therefore, music is the language of God. Music is a language more profound than words. How often have you heard a great piece of music and felt that? Great music does not just make you feel good; great music suggests some profound truth or mysterious meaning that is objectively true but not translatable into words. Attempts to translate music's meaning into words always fail. It is like trying to allegorize a symbol, trying to reduce to one literal, verbal meaning something that has many nonliteral, nonverbal meanings. Love fits this pattern: (1) it is not only subjective feeling but objective truth, (2) it is both mysterious and meaningful, and (3) its meaning is never reducible to words. The wooden trap of words can never capture the lobster of love, any more than a wooden "interpretation" of the meaning of a piece of music can capture the music itself.

I think music was the language in which God created the world. Both C. S. Lewis (in *The Magician's Nephew*) and J. R. R. Tolkien (in *The Silmarillion*) tell this story, and it goes back to a very old tradition, probably older than Pythagoras and his "music of the spheres". We moderns usually think of music as a later ornament added on to speech, but I suspect it is the opposite: speech is a later development from music. Song is not fancied poetry and poetry fancified prose; prose is ossified poetry and poetry ossified song. The reason I think this is because (1) "In the beginning, God", (2) "God is love", and (3) love is not a speech. We do not ever speak of "love speeches", only of "love songs".

Therefore, in the beginning was the Song of Songs. This book goes even farther back than Genesis, into the eternal heart of the Trinity.

2. Love Is the Greatest Song

Also in the title is the notion that love is not only a song but also the "song of songs", the greatest of songs. The Hebrew language has no superlative degree of comparison and uses instead this form: "greatest king" is "king of kings" and "greatest song" is "song of songs".

("Song of Solomon" is not the original title but the invention of modern editors. The original title, in the Hebrew Scriptures, is always the first verse, for these writings were scrolls, not books, and had no separate covers or title pages.)

What does it mean to call love the "greatest of songs"? Two things, at least. First, most obviously, it means love is the greatest in *value*. The poem itself says this, near the end: "If a man offered for love all the wealth of his house, it would be utterly scorned" (Song 8:7). Nothing can buy love because nothing is as precious as love; nothing can be exchanged for it. (This is also one reason why love must be free, as we will see later.) Song of Songs here anticipates 1 Corinthians 13: "The greatest of these is love."

But I think there is a second meaning implied, too: love is the greatest in *size*. The song of God that his creative love sings, that is, our lives, includes all other songs. Love is the meaning of the whole. We are all notes in God's symphony. When we listen only to our own note or to the few notes around us, it does not look like music or like love, but when we step back and look at the whole, everything falls into place as great music. Of course we are in no position to do this "stepping back" on our own power. How could we possibly get the God's-eye point of view? Only if God revealed it to us—as he has done here. Faith means believing this divine revelation. The man's-eye sharing in the God's-eye point of view is, precisely, the eye of faith.

The practical difference this image makes is immense. If you think you are making only meaningless noise, you are in Ecclesiastes' "vanity". If you think you are making music, you are in love. That is why Job is so dramatic: Job's question is ultimately: Am I only making noise, or am I making music? Am I in vanity, or am I in love?

A mythic image uses a part to symbolize the whole—for example, the earth is a great egg; the nine worlds grow from Yggdrasil, the cosmic ash tree; the world rests on the back of a giant turtle; life is a bowl of cherries—all these images seek to comprehend something of the whole by the symbolic use of the part. For we have no concept of the whole, of the meaning of everything, since concepts must always be defined and finite and set off from something else. The finite human mind can comprehend only finite concepts. But there is a way in which a finite, partial concept can mean or suggest the whole: by symbolism. The whole is something like an egg, or a tree, or a turtle, or a bowl of cherries. Thus Jesus constantly uses dramatic mythic images called parables to suggest the mysterious and indefinable but very real and definite "Kingdom of God": it is like a mustard seed, like a fishnet, like a fine pearl, like a vineyard. A picture is worth a thousand words, especially if it is a moving picture, a story. Somehow, these pictorial symbols can suggest more than they can say.

Now the fundamental question for Wisdom, for all three of

the Wisdom books we are exploring, is: What is human life, human existence? Ecclesiastes' answer was the dreaded word *vanity*, or nothingness, emptiness. Job knows life's meaning as suffering—but to what end, he does not find until the end. The answer of Song of Songs is that all of life is a love song. Every subatomic particle, from the Big Bang to the senility of the sun, is a note in this incredibly complex symphony. Every event, everything that has ever happened, the fall of every hair and every sparrow, is a theme in the surpassingly perfect melody of this song. But we who are in it do not hear or know it unless we are told by the Singer, who is outside it and who alone can know the point of the whole. Just as Pythagoras said we did not hear the "music of the spheres" for the same reason the blacksmith did not hear the hammering on the anvil: because he is too close to it, too used to it—so we do not hear the whole until we are outside the whole, after death; until we *are* whole, after death. In Heaven we will hear ourselves singing, that is, we will hear what we have sung.

3. Love Is Dialogue

The poem is in dialogue form, bride and groom singing to each other antiphonally, because love is essentially dialogue, and the form of a perfect poem manifests the content; the medium manifests the message.

There are only three ultimate messages, three possible philosophies of life. According to atheism, there is only the human monologue with no God to dialogue with. According to pantheism, there is only divine monologue with no created world of free souls for God to dialogue with. All is One. Only according to theism is there dialogue between Creator and creature. Only in theism does mankind confront an Other.

Thus the dialogue between lovers manifests a whole philosophy of life. It is no accident that love poetry blossoms more in theistic cultures than in atheistic or pantheistic ones.

The dialogue between male and female creatures reflects the dialogue *within* the Creator, the dialogue between Father and Son that eternally becomes the Holy Spirit. Life is dialogue ultimately because life is a reflection of God; and the very life of God, the eternal inner life of the Trinity, is the dialogue of love. We are meant to be with each other because God is eternally with-each-other; "each-otherness" reaches into the very heart of God. Otherness, plurality, individuality, society, and thus love are as ultimate as oneness. That is the thing pantheism fails to see: that to-be-with is the very nature of to-be; that relationship is not an accidental category and external addition, like time and place; that we must include in our list of "transcendentals" or universal properties of all being not only oneness but also manyness, not only sameness but also otherness, and not only truth and goodness and beauty but also love, at least in its most rudimentary form of the inherent tendency to-be-toward-another. The simplest conversation manifests the highest mystery.

4. Love Is Synergistic

There is no physical perpetual motion machine, but there is a spiritual perpetual motion machine: love. Love is perpetually reinforcing: the more we love, the more we are loved, and the more we are loved, the more we love. There is no necessary limit to this process. Even human love is potentially infinite, and divine love is actually infinite. There is no upper limit, no wall, to love. And there is no drag, no gravity built into love. When love wears down that is due to external friction, not internal friction: love itself has no tendency to wear down, only to increase.

We see this in the poem in the progression of the lyrics. The more each is loved by the other, the more he or she responds with increased love, and vice versa. After he says she is "as a lily among brambles" (Song 2:2), she responds that he is "as an apple tree among the trees" (Song 2:3); and after he declares, "behold, you are beautiful, my love" (Song 1:15), she echoes, "behold, you are beautiful, my beloved" (Song 1:16). They keep capping each other's lines because they keep reflecting each other's loves.

Love, being the fundamental spiritual force in the universe, transcends all other forces and their laws. It especially transcends the principle of physical entropy: its energy does not decrease but rather increases. That is why Heaven never gets boring. That is also the only way earth can conquer boredom, too.

5. Love Is Alive

We think of love as the product of things that are alive. Live animals put forth animal loves, live human beings put forth human loves, and the living God puts forth divine love. Even on the animal level, love tends to produce litters of new lives, but love is not a living thing in itself. But in God it is. It is the Holy Spirit. The love between Father and Son is so alive that it lives as a life of its own, a Person in its own right, the Third Person of the Trinity.

Now human loves resemble both the animal and the divine. To produce new living persons, our love needs the aid of biological reproduction, like the animals. But it also resembles the divine in that human love is alive. It is not literally another person, like the Holy Spirit, but it is more than a feeling in a person. We say we are "in love", not that love is in us. Why? All the myths saw love as a god or goddess, a real, living entity who could come into you and take over your life. Why? If we are old enough to remember the old Hollywood cliché, we say of love, "It's bigger than both of us." Why? If love is only a feeling confined to one person, these spontaneous expressions in our language and our cultural history are unexplainable. But if love is a real, living force, not only within us but between us, if we really are in love rather than love in us, then it is explainable. Love lives.

Thus all the images for love in the poem, as in most love poems, are images of living, growing things: a garden (Song 4:12, 16), a vineyard (Song 7:12; 8:11–12), a well of living water (Song 4:15). Love grows like a plant. It does not merely grow in us, with us, as a function of us; we grow in it, with it, as a function of it. It has a life of its own—ultimately because it is a seed of God planted in our lives. "He who lives in love, lives in God, and God in him" (1 Jn 4:16).

6. Love Is Gospel

Love is news, good news, Gospel. Love is promise of future bliss, hopeful of future reward, forward looking to future ratification. Its words always invite us forward. Even Freud perceived this: he divides the fundamental forces of the psyche into two: eros, the life force, drives us forward, while thanatos, the death force, the death wish, pulls us backward into the womb. For Freud life is the battle between these two forces. This is the residue or relic in the thought of the atheist and immoralist of the great Mosaic vision of life as the battle between the forces of life and death, obedience and disobedience to God:

> I call heaven and earth to witness against you this day, that I have set before you life and death, blessing and curse; therefore choose life, that you and your descendants may live, loving the Lord your God, obeying his voice, and cleaving to him (Dt 30:19–20).

The drama of Song of Songs, as of life, is the drama of choice between eros and thanatos, life and death, Yes and No as the two possible responses to the Gospel of the beloved. That Gospel speaks wonderful and mysterious promises. Will the human bride believe them? Will she have faith in her divine bridegroom? Will she choose life?

My beloved speaks and says to me,
Arise, my love, my fair one, and come away;
For lo, the winter is past, the rain is over and gone.
The flowers appear on the earth, the time of singing has
    come
And the voice of the turtledove is heard in our land.
The fig tree puts forth its figs, and the vines are in
    blossom,
They give forth fragrance.
Arise, my love, my fair one, and come away (Song
    2:10–13).

The response must be a "coming away" from the past, from death and darkness and the womb and sleep. In chapter 3, the bride is so sleepy that she does not respond to her beloved in time, and he leaves her to suffer and sorrow and search for him. Just as there is no sleep in Heaven (sleep being an image of death), there is no sleep in love. All the imagery in Song of Songs is morning imagery, not evening imagery: "The day breaks and the shadows flee away" (Song 2:17).

Love is Gospel because love is alive. Love is not an abstract ideal; love is a wedding invitation. Love is not something for us to approach; it is something that approaches us. We do not turn it on; it turns us on as a lamplighter turns on a lamp.

7. Love Is Power

Closely connected with love's livingness and love's Gospel-ness is love's power. The imagery in Song of Songs is startling. It is never weak and wimpy, sweet and swoony. The imagery is so strong and active that it is military. What woman has ever been flattered by her beloved's comparing her to an army and a fortress? This one has: "You are beautiful as Tizrah, my love, comely as Jerusalem, terrible as an army with banners" (Song 6:4). "Who is this that looks forth like the dawn, fair as the moon, bright as the sun, terrible as an army with banners"

(Song 6:10). It is the woman, not the man, who is being described here. The "terror" in "terrible" is not, of course, either the terror of disgust (as in "what a terrible rat-infested sewer!") or the terror of servile fear (as in "what a terrible thing a concentration camp is!") but the terror of awe (as in "Oz the Great and Terrible").

There is no chauvinistic passivity here. The bride is not a shrinking violet, nor does the groom want her to be. She is as active as he is but in a totally feminine way. She is the dawn, and the dawn "comes up like thunder" here. When God our groom comes to us with his love, we are not flattened but straightened, not turned off but turned on, not made passive but made active. The singing of the second part in a duet is just as active as the singing of the first part. We play second fiddle to God, but that is no fiddlin' around; that is fiddlin' up a storm. As we shall see later, love's power is so great that it is "strong as death" itself (Song 8:6).

8. Love Is Work

Love is not passive. Love is singing a duet, and that is work. Joyful work, but work nonetheless. Young lovers first fall in love passively, but if they are to stay in love they must actively work to keep it and grow it, like a seed that is first received into the ground but then must be tended and fertilized or it will die. Thus the bride sings, "I sought him whom my soul loves. . . . I will rise now and go about the city, in the streets and in the squares; I will seek him whom my soul loves" (Song 3:1–2). Life is a quest for love and a quest for God, and there is no car or plane for this trip. It is an old-fashioned quest made on our own two feet.

The most moving, beautiful, and enviable true-life love story I know in recent times is Sheldon Vanauken's *A Severe Mercy*. The question he is most often asked by his readers is how he and his wife achieved such a beautiful, intimate, and total love. It seemed too good to be true. We do not see such loves around us anymore. The modern world, though it talks incessantly about love, has almost totally murdered love. A stable marriage, much less a happy one, even less a joyful one, is the rarity, the exception, not the rule. What was Vanauken's secret?

His answer is surprisingly mundane: work. "We kept our love only because we worked at it." Love will not grow in modern fields without constant work. The soil is no longer rich. Perhaps the soil was never rich, but people used to be prepared to work at it. In any case, love can never last today unless the lovers are prepared for lifelong work. And that necessarily involves sacrifice—at least sacrifice of all the other things that you could be doing instead.

Work also requires patience—an increasingly rare commodity in our fast-food, instant-replay, live-for-the-present age. You cannot grow any fruit without patience. There are no instant apples.

Freud says that the two most basic needs everyone has are "love and work". That is a wise saying (though I think if he were asked to expand and explain it, Freud would not do so with equally wise sayings). And these two are one, for if work is to be fulfilling, it must be a work of love, and if love is to live, it must be a work. As Kierkegaard points out, love in Christianity is not a feeling, as it is for Romanticism; rather, "love is the works of love". That is why Christ can command love. Only a fool tries to command a feeling.

The strangest thing of all, perhaps, about our work of love is that it is both work and rest, both weekday and sabbath. Jesus made this clear when the Pharisees got angry at him for his work of healing on the sabbath. His answer told them, in effect, that you could no more stop this work than you could stop the sun from shining, for it is the very life of the Father, which eternally reaches out from the sabbath of eternity into the work week of time, as he did at the Creation. Jesus' answer to them was: "My Father is working still, and I am working"

(Jn 5:17). What has this to do with us human lovers? Everything, for a Christian's love is a participation in God's love through Christ the Mediator. Like Father, like Son; and like Christ, like Christian. Our work of love participates in the dual nature of Christ: divine and human, eternal and temporal, sabbath rest and weekday work, Easter Sunday and Good Friday.

9. Love Is Desire and Fulfillment

Another paradox of love is that it is bittersweet. Its very sweetness is bitter, and its very bitterness is sweet. Both qualities are present in desire. Love's desire, like all desire, is bitter and painful because it lacks what it wants. If it did not lack what it wanted, it would not be desiring it but would be enjoying it. But the very desire is also sweet, a joy, a fulfillment. Merely to long for God is better than to possess the whole world. This absence is better than any other presence; this desire is better than every other fulfillment.

Thus the bride's (the soul's) yearnings are put into the subjective mood, the mood of contrary-to-fact wishing: "O that you would kiss me with the kisses of your mouth, for your love is better than wine" (Song 1:2); "O that his left hand were under my head and that his right hand embraced me!" (Song 2:6). The desire is fulfilled only at the end of the poem (Song 8:5), but the desire itself is already a kind of fulfillment. The very longing for Heaven is Heaven.

Thus Dmitri Karamazov, in Dostoyevski's novel, tells God that if he should put him in Hell, he would sing to God the hymn of joy even from Hell, "the hymn from the underground". That would transform Hell (or the Siberian salt mines) into Heaven. The song of love makes Heaven. Heaven does not make God's love lovely; God's love makes Heaven heavenly.

No one has written about this longing better than C. S. Lewis, especially in *Surprised by Joy* and *The Pilgrim's Regress*.

Those are the books you should turn to if you want to explore deeper into this glorious, bottomless abyss.

10. Suffering Goes with Love

Love naturally suffers for the very obvious reason that it opens you up, exposes your tenderest, most vulnerable part, the quivering flesh of the heart, at the mercy of the beloved and of time and fate. If the beloved is human and not divine, you will always be betrayed. We always betray each other's love, in some way. That is what Original Sin means. No one is totally reliable. Put divine expectations on any human shoulders, even the shoulders of a saint, and you will be bitterly disappointed. And not only the beloved—time and fate and life itself seem to participate in Original Sin and the Fall, so that if there is one thing we can predict with accuracy, it is that "the course of true love never did run smooth". If you love, you will suffer. The only way to protect yourself against suffering is to protect yourself against love—and that is the greatest suffering of all, loneliness.

But in the very act of suffering, love can transform suffering, redeem it, and conquer it. Like a flood so powerful that no dam can stop it, like a flood that transforms the dam set up to stop its flow into a part of itself, as it carries the dam along downstream, so love transforms the suffering that at first seems set up against it into a part of itself. Thus in Song of Songs the bride refers to her suffering for love and the burn marks this suffering has made in her flesh as marks of beauty, not of ugliness:

> I am very dark, but comely, O daughters of Jerusalem;
> Like the tents of Kedar, like the curtains of Solomon.
> Do not gaze at me because I am swarthy,
> Because the sun has scorched me (Song 1:5–6).

The wounds of the resurrected Christ were not ugly but beautiful, like badges of glory, as they are in the stigmatized saints. So too the bride of Christ—the soul, the Church, the martyr (all Christians are martyrs)—is beautiful in her very suffering, as Christ was. The wrinkles around Mother Teresa's eyes are infinitely more beautiful than the makeup around a movie star's. Mother Angelica is more beautiful than Charlie's Angels.

Love increases the bride's suffering. She says, "I am sick with love" (Song 2:5). But her suffering only increases her love. For only after she comes up out of the wilderness (symbolic of suffering) in the last chapter does she attain three things she previously only longed for: trust, actual contact, and the consummation of her marriage:

> Who is that coming up from the wilderness,
> Leaning upon her beloved?
> Under the apple tree I awakened you (Song 8:5).

("Awakened" is a Hebrew euphemism for first intercourse with a virgin bride.)

It is as in Hosea 2: only after the wilderness, after suffering, is love perfected. Not only does love transform and perfect suffering; suffering also transforms and perfects love. The two things that seem to be enemies turn out to be mutually reinforcing allies. For only in the silence of the wilderness do we hear God's still, small voice whispering to the heart of our heart. C. S. Lewis says, in *The Problem of Pain*, "God whispers in our pleasures and shouts in our pains." That is true, but sometimes the opposite is also true. (See Hosea 2.)

11. Love Is Free

We all know this: love must be freely given and freely accepted. "It takes two to tango", and neither one can be pushed, pulled, dragged, or carried. There are really only three methods of influencing other people, three techniques of "behavior modification": pushing, carrying, or drawing. You can use force or

fear to push people where you want them to go, against their
will. Or you can carry them. Then they are passive and you do
the job for them, like a parent for an infant. Finally, you can
draw them, attract them, motivate them to move toward
you by the magnetism of desire. That is what the bride asks
the groom to do: "Draw me after you, let us make haste"
(Song 1:4). She will not be his slave and be pushed, or his child
and be carried, but his bride and be drawn. He has the initiative,
but she responds with equal freedom and equal value. To be
drawn is as free a choice as to draw. To come is as free as to say,
"Come".

Even God cannot change this, for it is the inner law of love's
nature, which is his own nature, and God cannot change his
own nature. So even God cannot love and force at the same
time. God cannot force us to love him. The one thing even
God cannot give himself is our love. God can create a universe,
but God cannot create love in us, only elicit it from us. For
love is not a creature, a thing created, like a universe. A thing
created is passive. The universe did nothing to help itself get
created. But love is active, not passive; free, not forced; from
within, not without. It grows like fruit, by its own inner
mystery. Thus the groom says repeatedly throughout the
poem,

> I adjure you,
> O daughter of Jerusalem,
> By the gazelles
> or the hinds of the field,
> that you stir not up nor awaken love
> until it please (Song 3:5).

It is the hardest thing in the world to be patient about, for it
is the thing we need the most and desire the most. But it is also
the most necessary thing in the world to be patient about, for if
it is not free, it is not love.

People talk a lot about freedom today, much more so than in
ancient times. Perhaps that is because they do not know love.

For lovers do not talk about freedom: they are free already. They do not desire to be free; they desire to be bound forever to their beloved. To be free from love, free from God, is precisely Hell.

12. Love Is True to Reality

"Rightly do they love you" (Song 1:4), says the bride. Love is not only the supreme value but also the supreme truth. It is not only fulfilling to me but also fulfilling reality. Love is ontologically right. It is realistic; it is conformity to reality; it is living in the real world. We have this horrible habit of speaking as if love were a mere ideal and "reality" or "the real world" were a loveless, ugly, hard-bitten thing—in other words, as if people determined reality, and the worst people at that. No, people do not determine reality; reality determines people. Reality is not simply what people make or do; reality is what God is and does. And God is love. Love is therefore the central law of reality, and when we love, we conform to reality.

This is especially true when we love God. This point refers to the bride's (soul's) love of the groom (God); *that* is the supreme realism. The next point will be much more surprising: that God's love for us is also realism, in fact, perfect accuracy.

13. Love Is Accurate

Love is more accurate than mathematics. We think and say, in our shallowness, that "love is blind". It is exactly the opposite: it is the supreme vision, the supreme wisdom, the supreme enlightenment. God is love, and God is not blind; therefore, love is not blind. If love is blind, then either God is not love, or God is blind.

When we say "love is blind", we may be thinking of selfish

love, or animal love, or puppy love. That may be blind. But agape is not blind. We must be sure about this truth, because it will be severely tested by some startling verses in Song of Songs. When we read these verses, we will be tempted to jettison the whole symbolic interpretation, for it seems that the things the groom says to the bride could not possibly be said by God to the sinful human soul. For instance, he says in Song of Songs 4:7, "Behold, you are all fair, my love. There is no flaw in you." But there are plenty of flaws in us, and we know that, and God says that in many other passages of Scripture. This sounds like a denial of sin. It sounds as if love is blind indeed.

In another passage, the groom addresses his blushing bride, who is hiding in a rock, probably because she is ashamed of her ugliness compared with his beauty. The groom says,

> O my dove,
> in the clefts of the rock,
> in the covert of the cliff,
> Let me see your face,
> let me hear your voice.
> For your voice is sweet
> and your face is comely (Song 2:14).

She probably thinks her face is as comely as a barn door and her voice as sweet as a crow's. The question is: Who is right? She thinks she is ugly; he thinks she is beautiful. If he is God, he must be right. "Let God be true and every man a liar" (Rom 3:4). But how can this be?

The world's second greatest love poem poses the same problem. No woman has ever been so exalted in verse as Beatrice by Dante, especially in the "Vita Nuova". Not Virgil, Dante's ideal, the world's greatest poet, but Beatrice leads Dante out of Purgatory in the *Divine Comedy*. Dante, like God, says to his beloved that she is all fair, that she is a goddess, that she is the glory of God shining on a human face, that she is not a thing in the world but a hole to another world through which Dante can see the divine light. God is the sun, and Beatrice is the moon. What is going on here?

The historian is tempted to reply to that question by doing some historical research into the "real" Beatrice. He would find out that Beatrice was a teenaged Florentine girl whom Dante knew from an early age, that she was the daughter of a merchant in town, that no one ever thought of her as remarkably beautiful, and that Dante just happened to see her passing under his window one day and suddenly was caught up in the vision, as if his life had turned a corner as Beatrice turned the corner of his street. "Here begins the new life", Dante wrote. But all that happened was that he saw her face. As in the hokey old song "Stranger in Paradise", Dante said, in effect,

> I saw her face
> and I ascended
> Out of the commonplace
> into the rare.
> Somewhere in space
> I hang suspended.

Is this sight or sickness? The psychologist, rushing to the aid of the historian, now chimes in, patronizingly, "We understand what is happening here. It's projection. Dante was in love with love, and Beatrice just happened by at the right time. Dante projected the depth and beauty of his own heart onto Beatrice. 'Beauty is in the eye of the beholder', and Dante's poetic eyes are full of beauty. Just as when you have yellow jaundice in your eye, the world looks yellow, so when you have Dante's beauty, the first person to come into view looks beautiful. It's not Beatrice that's beautiful; it's Dante."

If Dante were to hear that, I think he would challenge both the historian and the psychologist to a duel to the death to defend the honor of his beloved Beatrice. But more importantly, supposing that they all survived the duel, he would challenge them to a debate. He would insist that his love had perfect accuracy, objectivity, and realism; that he was right and they were wrong; that he was not projecting at all; that it was Beatrice, not Dante, who was surpassingly beautiful; and that he, Dante, contributed only the receptors for this beauty. He is a great poet, and a great poet is a great seer. He sees what is. He has X-ray vision. The rest of the world may agree with the historian and the psychologist and see only ordinariness in Beatrice, but Dante sees beneath the caterpillar into the butterfly —the butterfly that is really there in Beatrice, the butterfly that *is* Beatrice.

Could Dante be right? Of course he is right, and you know it. Who knows you better, the world's greatest psychologist who only wants to use you as a case study, or your best friend who is not very bright but cares about you deeply? It is no contest. Only love has eyes. To understand the world of things, you need science and suspicion and the method of doubt: accept nothing until it is proved. Every idea is guilty until proved innocent. But to know people, you need the opposite method: trust, love, openness. Persons are innocent until proved guilty. You cannot hear them unless that is your attitude. Suspicion never reaches the other's heart.

So Dante is right. Beatrice really is a goddess. And so are Helen, and Mary, and Leslie, and Jo Ann, but they do not have Dante-like poets with X-ray vision to tell them that. Ah, but they do. Their poet speaks in Song of Songs. Their poet is God.

What God says is true, and you had better believe it. What happens if you do? Suppose Robert Redford came up to you, who think of yourself as a Plain Jane, and said, "You are the woman I've been looking for all my life. You move me to tears, you are so beautiful. I want to marry you and make you happy forever." Would you think of yourself a little differently? Well, if even Robert Redford can change your dull self-image, cannot God do it also? Dare you call yourself a Plain Jane if it means calling God a liar? One of you is wrong. You say you are ugly; God says you are beautiful. If you are right, God is wrong. That just cannot be. The alternative is that God is right and you are wrong. You are not ugly. You are beautiful. What God says is fact, objective truth, utter reality.

But what about sin? Does God just hide his eyes? How can that be realism? God does not hide his eyes. *Your* eyes are hidden in time, hidden from your eternal destiny and identity. You see only the present crude sketch of yourself. He sees the completed masterpiece, for he sees from eternity. Your life is like a string pulled taut. Like an ant, you crawl along the string of your lifetime, from one end (birth) to the other (death). But God sees the whole string end on, from the end. He blinks at nothing; he sees everything in its true perspective. He sees your whole life, but not as you do, piecemeal. He sees you whole, as you see a finished painting. And the judgment he pronounces on you is "perfect".

That is our destiny, according to Christ: "You must be perfect as your heavenly Father is perfect." The Christ who says this incredible thing is also the Christ who alone makes it happen, the Savior, the Way. The Way will have his way. We are to be "all fair" as he is all fair. Contentment with anything less than perfection is our way, perhaps, but not his. For he is love, and love (according to George Macdonald) is "easy to please but hard to satisfy". Thank God for both of those facts!

14. Love Is Simple

The style of the poetry in Song of Songs is amazingly simple, even though the content suggested is amazingly complex. Though the greatest minds of theologians, saints, and mystics can explore the depths of this book for hundreds of pages without coming close to exhausting its riches, yet its point is so simple that only the simplest, haikulike poetry suffices:

> Behold, you are beautiful, my love,
> Behold, you are beautiful;
> Your eyes are doves.

Behold, you are beautiful, my beloved,
Truly lovely;
Our couch is green (Song 1:15–16)

To a nonlover this is supremely trite and boring. To a lover it is perfect, like a diamond. To a nonlover it is endless repetition. To a lover it can go on forever, like God himself, one, perfect, self-sufficient, "the one thing needful". If you have ever fallen in love or had a friend who did, you know the difference between these two perspectives. The lover is totally engrossed in his love, or rather in his beloved. He is never bored. He could go on and on forever. The outside observer, however—the friend, roommate, or family member —finds the lover supremely boring, narrow, obsessed—exactly the opposite of what he is to himself.

Imagine the nonlover as literary critic evaluating the little poem above. "Behold, you are beautiful, my love"—you cannot get more trite and clichéish than that. Totally unoriginal. You could not imagine a less imaginative sentence. "Behold, you are beautiful"—the second line is even less original than the first. Nothing but repetition. We already know she is beautiful; stop harping on it. "Your eyes are doves"—silly, simplistic image. Does not even fit. Oh, well: love is blind. Let us see what he says; maybe he is a better poet than she was, at least. "Behold, you are beautiful, my beloved." Oh, no! Not more of the same! All he does is repeat her words. "Truly lovely"—again and again. Four out of five lines totally dispensable. "Our couch is green"—who cares? Certainly I do not. This is the silliest, simplest, tritest, most childish poem (if you dare dignify it by that name) I have ever read.

But now listen to the real critics, the lovers themselves. "Behold"—how startling the vision of love is! What a surprise —like the Beatific Vision, like the Light of God suddenly appearing to human eyes! "You are beautiful, my love"— exactly right, true, essential. Nothing more need be said. This is heart's desire; this is all the human heart hungers for. The very simplicity is perfect eloquence. "Behold, you are beautiful" —like the Word of God reflecting the Father perfectly, the second line reflects the first, and for the same reason: you cannot get any better than that. "Your eyes are doves"—a simple but mysterious fittingness to this image satisfies the heart even while the mind is puzzled. For only the heart can understand simple things; the mind plays another game, constructing truth laboriously out of concepts. "Behold, you are beautiful, my beloved"—she can do no better than perfection, so her response is in kind, reflective of the perfection and simplicity of his love. "Truly lovely"—how wonderful that she never gets tired of this central fact! "Our couch is green" —every detail of both art and nature is now newly lit up with the light and beauty of love. Every leaf, every bed, every bird sings the same song, the very song of God, the One, the single-minded Lover of the whole universe in all its wonderfully diverse parts. Why, a whole world view is implied in these lines!

You see, though love is not content with anything less than perfection (as we saw in our last point) and with its own perfection, yet with that it is quite content and needs nothing more. And love experiences something of that heavenly perfection even now on earth, in prophetic form. Therefore it is content even now. Though the seed of love is not yet grown, it is already sown, and it is the best seed, the all-sufficient seed, the one and only perfect seed, "the pearl of great price" worth selling worlds for. We do right to be satisfied with it rather than looking for anything else.

15. Love Is Individual

The object of love is a person, and every person is an individual. No person is a class, a species, or a collection. There is no such thing as the love of humanity because there is no such thing as humanity. If your preachers or teachers have told you that the Bible teaches you to love humanity, they have told you a lie. Not once does the Bible say that; not once does it even mention the word *humanity*. Jesus always commands us to love God and our neighbor instead.

How comfortable "humanity" is! "Humanity" never shows up at your door at the most inconvenient time. "Humanity" is not quarrelsome, alcoholic, or fanatical. "Humanity" never has the wrong political, religious, and sexual opinions. "Humanity" is never slimy, swarmy, smarmy, smelly, or smutty. "Humanity" is so ideal that one could easily die for it. But to die for your neighbor, to die for Sam Slug or Mehetibel Crotchit—unthinkable. Except for love.

One of the saints said that if you had been the only person God ever created, he would have gone to all the trouble he went to just to save you alone. When he died on the Cross, he did not die for humanity; he died for you. "Behold, I have called you by name", he says. "I have engraven your name upon my palm." When he welcomes you into your heavenly mansion, he will not address you as "comrade". Lovers love to whisper each other's names because the name stands for the person, the individual.

Thus in Song of Songs the chorus of nonlovers wonders,

> What is your beloved more than another beloved,
> O fairest among women? (Song 5:9).

And she replies,

> My beloved is all radiant and ruddy,
> Distinguished among ten thousand (Song 5:10).

The same is true of her from his viewpoint:

> There are sixty queens and eighty concubines,
> and maidens without number.
> My dove, my perfect one, is only one (Song 6:8–9).

God's name is the uniquely individual word *I* (Ex 3:14). God's image in us is our I. That this private, unique, individual thing can be nevertheless shared is the apparent contradiction of love.

The lover sees the beloved not as one among many but as the center of the universe; not as an ingredient but as a whole; not on the periphery of his mind's circle but at the center, standing at the same place as himself, his own center, his own uniquely individual I. Love has two I's; that is why it sees so well.

Why did God create you? He created billions of other people; were they not enough for him? No, they were not. He had to have you. He will not rest until he has you home. Even if you are the one sheep that is lost, he will leave the ninety-nine (or ninety-nine billion) others to seek you wherever you are. He will come into your thickets and your wilderness and your suffering and even, on the Cross, your sin. "For our sake he made him to be sin who knew no sin, so that in him we might become the righteousness of God" (2 Cor 5:21). One of the splinters on the Cross that pierced his flesh was yours alone. And one of the gems in his crown will be yours alone. For here is how your divine lover sees you:

> As a lily among brambles
> So is my love among maidens (Song 2:2).

And your response must be just as individual to him:

> As an apple tree among the trees of the wood,
> So is my beloved among young men (Song 2:3).

That is what it means to obey "the first and greatest commandment", to love the Lord your God with your whole heart. "For the Lord your God is a jealous God." Love is jealous because love is individual. Love will not share the beloved with another, as if a heart could be divided into parts. That is why God must be infinite: so that he can give his whole heart to each of us without being divided. Only infinity can do that. We can give our whole heart only to one at a time: to one God, because there is only one, and to one spouse. Marriage is earth's closest image for Heaven because it is all or nothing, forever—a leap of faith.

16. Love Is All Conquering

"*Amor vincit omnia*", love conquers all, says the poet. No force on earth can withstand its power, for its power is divine. The mountains, scripturally symbolic of obstacles (see Is 40:4), are no obstacle to love in Song of Songs; the beloved "comes leaping upon the mountains, bounding over the hills" (Song 2:8). Like faith, love moves mountains (see Mt 17:20). In fact, the very obstacles in love's way become transformed by love into a part of itself. Onerous tasks become opportunities for heroism. As the priest tells the marrying couple in the Catholic marriage ceremony, marriage is so high and holy, so demanding of self-sacrifice, that "only love can make it possible, and only perfect love can make it a joy".

Love's enemies darken the horizon of our fallen world, and like the Old Testament prophet we naturally cry out in complaint to God. But he shows us here the vision, as he showed the prophet, of greater armies still, the armies of the Lord, bright with angelic clarity and charity, surrounding the dark host of Israel's enemies that in turn surround little, beleaguered Israel. We are never alone. "Lo, I am with you always, even to the end of the world"—thus spoke the only one who ever truly said what all the Hitlers, Napoleons, Alexanders, and Caesars longed to say: "I have overcome the world" (Jn 16:33). They failed because their weapons were hate. He succeeded because his weapon was love. They slew their enemies; he let himself be slain. The Lamb conquered even the Dragon (in Revelation) by the blood of his love. The wounds of the sacred heart of Jesus are the most powerful force in the universe. If our love is united to his, if we are united to him, we and our love *cannot* fail.

17. Love Is a Surprise

Love is not calculated, controlled, predicted, or expected. Love is a "good catastrophe" (to use Tolkien's neologism). It is the mark of God's presence, and so it takes us by surprise, as he does. The God of the Bible, as distinct from any of the many gods of the human imagination, is not the point of any human triangle; we are the point of his triangle. He is not the target of the arrows of our spirit; we are the target of his arrows. The God of the philosophers is simply "Being", but the God of Abraham, Isaac, and Jacob creeps up behind us and says, "Boo!"

That is why the poet uses the strange-sounding image of the gazelle. God the gazelle? Yes. Have you ever seen a gazelle? He hops about with incredible lightness and unpredictability, like a magnified flea. His very standing there seems active, almost threatening—as if he is every moment threatening to leap at you. Thus the bride is suddenly surprised by his voice:

> The voice of my beloved!
> Behold, he comes,
> Leaping upon the mountains,
> Bounding over the hills.
> My beloved is like a gazelle,
> Or a young stag.
> Behold, there he stands
> Behind our wall,
> Gazing in at the windows,
> Looking through the lattice.
> My beloved speaks and says to me:
> Arise, my love, my fair one,
> And come away (Song 2:8–10).

Love elopes. God calls us, as he called Abraham, away from the security we knew, out of our old, familiar, little room, down the ladder of faith and into his arms. Jesus called his disciples that way—just as a lover elopes with his beloved. Whenever we think we have got him planned, he blows away our plans like the clouds of smoke they are, and stands in front of us in place of our dreams, our cloudy expectations, and forces us to choose between him and ourselves, between the

God of surprises and the idol of same old self, between God the gazelle and Self the slug. It is ultimately the choice between Heaven and Hell.

18. Love Is Fearless

"There is no fear in love, but perfect love casts out fear", says John the evangelist (1 Jn 4:18). Solomon the evangelist says the same. Love and fear are like oil and water: they cannot occupy the same space, the same soul, at the same time. One casts out the other.

In Song of Songs, the bride is hiding in the cleft of the rock (Song 2:14), fearful of meeting her beloved. This is not silly; indeed, the typically modern absence of fear is silly. It is simply not true that "there is nothing to fear but fear itself". There is plenty to fear. There is evil, for one thing, and Hell, and Satan. And there is the wrath of God, which is *not* a crude, superstitious myth unless the Bible is a crude, superstitious myth. On a human level, there is the terrible but very real possibility that the beloved will not freely return our love. Love is terribly vulnerable, easily misunderstood or rejected. There is plenty to fear.

Most of all, there is goodness to fear. God is perfect goodness, absolute holiness, perfect righteousness. Is *that* fearsome? It certainly is—to a soul not wholly in love with goodness, not wholly confirmed in righteousness, not 100 percent on the side of holiness. Would you feel quite *comfortable* meeting God right now, this very minute, face to face, with no hiding, no excuses, and nothing about you unrevealed? If you can answer Yes to that terrible invitation, you are either the world's greatest saint or the world's greatest fool.

It is good that there be fear so that love can cast it out. If there is no fear for love to cast out, love falls on unprepared soil. If your concept of God lacks awe, circumspection, fear, and trembling, then your concept of love will also lack awe. If your soul is so small and arrogant that it feels comfortable and cuddly with God, then the only size love you will admit into your soul is a comfortable and cuddly love.

But once the great and rightful fear is there, the great and rightful love takes its place. Fear is a bond, however childish, between the soul and God. Love is a more perfect and intimate bond. Nothing less than the greater bond should cast out the lesser bond. "Experts" in pastoral psychology and "religious education" should not be allowed to steal that precious seed, for when the seed of fear falls into the ground of love and dies, it brings forth much fruit.

Love casts out fear because the kind of love we are talking about here is agape, not eros. Desire does not cast out fear, but agape does, because agape includes trust. Only trust, only faith, overcomes fear. If we think our love will be rejected, we fear. But if we trust our beloved to be also our lover, if we know our love will be reciprocated or even topped, we have no fear. "There is no fear *in* love", only outside it.

And God's love is the only totally trustable love (thus the only love guaranteed to cast out fear) because only God totally knows, accepts, and affirms us. "Even if my mother and my father forsake me, the Lord will lift me up" (Ps 27:10).

19. Love Is Exchange of Selves

Something extremely simple yet incredibly mysterious is said in Song of Songs 2:16 and again at 7:10: "My beloved is mine and I am his." Love exchanges selves. When I love you, I no longer possess myself; you do. I have given it away. But I possess your self. How can this be? How can the gift of the giver be the very giver? How can the hand that gives hold itself in itself as its own gift? The ordinary relationship between giver and gift, subject and object, cause and effect, is overcome here. The simple-sounding truism that in love you give your very self to your beloved is a high and holy mystery.

Its ultimate explanation is an even higher and holier mystery, the Trinity itself. Lovers belong to each other because love is the nature of God, and the Persons in the Divine Trinity give themselves to each other. The Son *is* the very Word, or thought, or mind of the Father given so totally that he is another Person; and the Spirit *is* the very love between Father and Son given so totally that he too eternally becomes a Third Person.

The image of this ultimate Fact in human love is that lovers can really give themselves to each other, so that "the two become one" without ceasing to be two. Already in human love the laws of mathematics are transcended: a powerful clue that we should not expect them to apply to divine love, a good piece of evidence that it would be arrogant folly to deny the doctrine of the Trinity because it does not make mathematical sense.

In the Trinity, God eternally becomes one by knowing and loving himself. It is the union among the three Persons that is God's highest unity, not the mathematical oneness or identity of his essence. That is why among us, too, as his image, the unity between lover and beloved is closer than the unity between the lover and himself. He is more one with his beloved; he finds his oneness, his unique selfhood, his identity, more in her than in himself; he "identifies" more with her than with himself.

And as the Persons of the Trinity become one and as husband and wife become one, so God and man become one, too, in Christ. God's love exchanges his self with our self. He puts us into his own mystical Body. He puts his own Spirit into us. He is in us, and we are in him. Someone said that if theologians only fully understood the word *in*, they would have solved all mysteries.

Mystery though this is, it is not remote. Any lover knows it. Slaves belong to their masters out of force and convention, and yuppies belong only to themselves, but lovers belong to each other. Thus, if I love you, wherever you are, I am, for I am more with you than with myself. Whatever happens to you happens to me; thus it happens to you twice: to you in you and to you in me. That is why a loving father who spanks his deserving child speaks literal truth when he says, "This hurts me more than it hurts you." And perhaps that is also how it is when God punishes us.

20. Love Is Triumphalistic

Much of the imagery in the Song of Songs does not appeal to modern sensibilities because it is old-fashionedly triumphalistic, ceremonial, formal, even military. For instance,

> What is that coming up from the wilderness,
> like a column of smoke,
> perfumed with myrrh and frankincense,
> with all the fragrant powders of the merchant?
> Behold, it is the litter of Solomon!
> About it are sixty mighty men
> of the mighty men of Israel,
> all girt with swords
> and experts in war,
> each with his sword at his thigh,
> against alarms by night.
> King Solomon made himself a palanquin
> from the wood of Lebanon.
> He made its posts of silver,
> its back of gold, its seat of purple;
> it was lovingly wrought within
> by the daughters of Jerusalem.
> Go forth, O daughters of Zion,
> and behold King Solomon,
> with the crown with which his mother crowned him
> on the day of his wedding,
> on the day of the gladness of his heart (Song 3:6–11).

This impresses us much less than it did the ancients because we live in a flat world, an egalitarian world, while the ancients lived in a world full of spiritual heights and hierarchies, a world of spires and turrets. But our hearts protest against our flatland and yearn for their true country, their true dimension of verticality. Love is, simply, superior. It belongs on a throne. It rightly brags, praises, exults, celebrates, sings its Song of Songs, its nonordinary song, its Greatest Song. It deserves silver and gold and robes and crowns. Heaven will be full of it (if the symbolism in Revelation means anything at all); had we not better practice living with it?

21. Love Is Natural

Love is supernatural, but love is also natural—like Christ, who is both fully God and fully man. Love is not only natural, the fulfillment of human nature, the point of the divine design for man; love is also the fundamental force in nature. Gravity is only love turned inside out, love on a physical plane. Love "moves the sun and all the stars", as Dante and the ancients knew. Love is the leitmotif of nature's symphonic suite, the theme of nature's song.

That is why the poet of Song of Songs, like all traditional love poets, finds and uses analogies throughout nature for human love. If love were not already the guiding thread of nature, it would be artificial and an act of spiritual violence to use natural images for it.

Modern sensibilities are more materialistic than those of the ancients, however, and so we need to be reeducated into at least one crucial feature of traditional imagery. These images are often based not on an empirical, visible likeness but on an emotional likeness. Consider the following passage, for instance. Not one of the seven natural images is one of visible resemblance, except very remotely. If the reader thinks the writer is attempting that, the spell of the poetry not only will not work but also will work a counterspell of scorn and laughter. But if the reader understands that subtle and multiple

storys of emotional equivalence are built onto only a small
foundation of visible equivalence, he will be able to enter into
the poet's secret world of fittingness.

> Your eyes are doves
> behind your veil.
> You hair is like a flock of goats,
> moving down the slopes of Gilead.
> Your teeth are like a flock of shorn ewes
> that have come up from the washing,
> all of which bear twins,
> and not one among them is bereaved.
> Your lips are like a scarlet thread,
> and your mouth is lovely.
> You cheeks are like halves of a pomegranate
> behind your veil.
> Your neck is like the tower of David,
> built for an arsenal,
> whereon hang a thousand bucklers,
> all of them shields for warriors.
> Your breasts are like two fawns,
> twins of a gazelle,
> that feed among the lilies (Song 4:1–5).

Just *how* it is fitting to compare breasts to lily-feeding fawns
is much harder to analyze and explain than to intuit; but *that* it
is fitting, that there is a natural fit between what love sees in the
beloved and in nature, is the more important point. Nature
imagery is everywhere in love poetry because love is everywhere in nature. Everything in nature can symbolize love
because everything in nature was designed and created to
manifest the God of love. "The heavens are telling the glory of
God and the firmament proclaims his handiwork" (Ps 19:1).
Every blade of grass is a blade of grace, a grace note in God's
single Song. Nature is not blind and dumb. Nature is eloquent.
Human science is blind and dumb if it does not hear this
eloquence.

22. Love Is Faithful

Each of the Ten Commandments is a specification of love: love does not steal, love takes a sabbath, love does not bear false witness, and so on. The one exception seems to be adultery. But it is not love that commits adultery against itself. Love does not adulterate itself. Love needs no external law to force it to be faithful; true love is naturally true. Love wants to be faithful. It wants to give all of itself to one, not to disperse and divide itself upon many.

Thus, "a garden locked is my sister, my bride; a garden locked, a fountain sealed" (Song 4:12). Love is sealed against intruders: "Set me as a seal upon your heart" (Song 8:6).

It is impossible to give the whole of your self to more than one person, for you can give the whole only to the whole, and only an individual person is a whole. A group is not a whole. You cannot give the whole of yourself to a group of two or more. If you multiply the recipient, you divide the gift—and the giver. And a divided giver, a divided self, is a terrible thing, like a split personality. Only God can give the whole of himself to more than one, to each one of us, one at a time, because God is in eternity and has all of time at his disposal. No one can give all to more than one at a time, but we are in time, and God is not.

Though God loves each of us, his love for each one is just as jealous and sealed and faithful as ours. The divine husband will no more share his bride, your soul, with others than a human husband will. Instead, he will "husband" his resource, his possession, to himself. "For I the Lord your God am a jealous God" (Ex 20:5). Surely there is a connection between modernity's scorn of this "jealousy" in God and its scorn of fidelity in marriage. We have exchanged the "narrow way" of Christ for an ecumenical orgy, a "group grope" among gods; and we have exchanged the unadulterated, undivorceable "what God has joined together, let not man put asunder" for history's most catastrophic breakdown of mankind's most fundamental institution. The two exchanges are two sides of the same profitless coin, and "what does it profit a man if he gain the whole world and lose his own soul?"

23. Love Is Ready

When the angel appeared to Mary, she was ready with her response: Yes, Fiat, let it be, "Be it done unto me according to your word." That is why Mary is the perfect saint: a perfect saint has perfect love, and perfect love is perfectly ready with its simple Yes.

But the bride in Song of Songs, like our own soul, is not perfectly ready. She makes excuses, and because of this fear, withdrawal, or double-mindedness, the longed-for consummation of their love is postponed, and she suffers immeasurably:

> I slept, but my heart was awake.
> Hark! My beloved is knocking.
> "Open to me, my sister, my love,
> my dove, my perfect one;
> for my head is wet with dew,
> my locks with the drops of the night."
> I had put off my garment,
> how could I put it on?
> I had bathed my feet,
> how could I soil them?
> My beloved put his hand to the latch,
> and my heart was thrilled within me.
> I arose to open to my beloved,
> and my hands dripped with myrrh,
> my fingers with liquid myrrh,
> upon the handles of the bolt.
> I opened to my beloved,
> but my beloved had turned and gone.

My soul failed me when he spoke.
I sought him, but found him not;
I called him, but he gave no answer.
The watchmen found me,
as they went about in the city;
they beat me, they wounded me,
they took away my mantle,
those watchmen of the walls.
I adjure you, O daughters of Jerusalem,
if you find my beloved,
that you tell him
I am sick with love (Song 5:2–8).

We are always doing that with God. The divinely whispered invitation to turn immediately to him, to follow the first breath of his Spirit, is seldom heeded. When we have more time, when we are in a better mood, when these Martha-like many things are taken care of, then we can attend to the Mary thing, the "one thing needful". But tomorrow never comes, and if we do not turn today we simply do not turn, for today is the only time there ever is. "Now is the time of salvation." In postponing the soul's simple, central sacrifice of all else and turning to God with open eyes, open heart, and open hands, we postpone the fullness of salvation. For that is what salvation is: receiving God into our soul, our will, in the living present. The living God does not enter into anything dead. The past is dead, and the future is not yet born. God lives in the present and enters the present only.

Did you ever realize how hard it is to do the thing so many popular psychologies tell you so glibly to do: to live in the present? I will show you how hard this is. I dare you to stop reading right now, to stop hoping for something valuable to come to you in the next sentence, and to turn to God immediately and tell him how you love him and let him tell you how he loves you—right now. Be wiser than the bride in the Song.

Are you back? Was that not the best part of the book? Or did you cheat and just think about doing it? You had better not plan on getting to Heaven that way: by thinking about it.

24. Love Is All Inclusive

The love this Song sings is inclusive of all loves. All four of "the four loves" are here. (For an excellent introduction to the four loves, see C. S. Lewis' book by that title.) For in that most complete and most intimate of all human relationships, marriage as God planned it, there are all four loves; and in the marriage between God and the soul there are also all four loves. Neither the earthly nor the heavenly marriage is an alternative to other loves, exclusive of other loves. Both are all inclusive. Thus Saint Augustine says in the *Confessions* that he who has God has everything, and he who has God and nothing else lacks nothing, and he who has God and everything else does not have anything more than he who has God alone.

We find first of all eros, or desire, in Song of Songs. In fact, we find ravishment—but the deeper and more passionate ravishment of the heart, which is capable of much more passion, intimacy, and joy than the flesh only: "You have ravished my heart, my sister, my bride, you have ravished my heart with a glance of your eyes" (Song 4:9). "Under the apple tree I awakened you" (Song 8:5)—desire is consummated. "Its flashes are flashes of fire, a most vehement flame" (Song 8:6).

We find also affection here. In fact, we find this most tender and comfortable love juxtaposed with the most passionate love in Song of Songs 4:9, where the bride is addressed as both "my sister" and "my bride". The juxtaposition continues in Song of Songs 4:10, 4:12, and 5:1. A marriage made wholly of the fire of eros with none of the surrounding walls of affection would not be livable for long.

Third, we find here also friendship: "This is my beloved and

this is my friend" (Song 5:16). (Friendship differs from affection in that it is freely entered into and deliberate, while
affection is a spontaneous feeling. Also, affection does not
require equality; friendship does.)
Finally, we find charity and self-giving: "I am my beloved's"
(Song 7:10); "My beloved is mine and I am his" (Song 2:16). If
any one of these four love ingredients is missing in marriage,
the marriage is not only incomplete but also endangered. All
four are also present in and perfected by the divine marriage,
for nature reflects grace, and grace perfects and redeems nature
rather than abolishing her. The horizontal marriage between
groom and bride reflects the principles of the vertical marriage
between grace and nature. That is the deep mystery of marriage
Saint Paul reveals in Ephesians 5:21–33.

25. Love Is "Sexist"

The very word *sexist* is a bad word, both because it is pre-
judicial (confusing a description with a value judgment) and
because it implies a confusion between "inherently different"
and "inherently superior". My friend Sheldon Vanauken claims
to have been the inventor of the word during his "silly sixties"
phase, for which he now feels deep regret. (See *Under the
Mercy*.) Perhaps this paragraph can do a tiny bit to shorten his
Purgatory. Love contains an inherent polarity and differentiation
between the sexes but not an inherent chauvinism. That is how
love is "sexist", and it is reflected throughout the Song of
Songs.
The mystics say that to God all souls are feminine. Not
female but feminine. Male and female are confined to the
biological, but masculine and feminine extend further, into
souls as well as bodies. Here is the proof. Only a Cartesian
dualist could deny the soul-body unity, and no one could deny
that bodies are inherently male or female. Put these two
premises together, and you get the conclusion that something

parallel to male and female is to be expected in the soul: masculine and feminine. To each other, we are masculine or feminine. To God we are all feminine. The very word for "soul" is feminine in every major Western language except English, which alone is "desexed", that is, has nouns without gender.

In the Song of Songs it must be the groom and not the bride who symbolizes God, the bride and not the groom who symbolizes the soul. The reason for this "sexism" is not that male is superior but that when God touches us he performs the male, not the female, function, analogically: he impregnates the soul, not vice versa. That is the deepest reason why throughout the Bible the human image for God is male, never female. It is only an image, of course, and not literal; God has no body and thus no biological sex at all. But the image images something, and that something is the relationship that the inventors of these images experienced: they all experienced God as the husband of the soul. The fact that God spiritually impregnates us and not vice versa, the fact that God creates new life in us and not vice versa, and the fact that God comes into us and not vice versa, cannot be changed any more than the fact that a man impregnates a woman and not vice versa can be changed. No matter how much we rant and rave, we cannot change the essential, eternal laws of the very structure of reality to conform to our latest ideological fashions and fancies.

26. Love Is as Strong as Death

Finally, love cannot be defeated even by death. Love is the only thing that can stand up to death. Death removes everything else. Even the stars are subject to death. But billions of years from now, when all the stars in the universe have died, love will still be alive, and if we live in love, if we identify ourselves with love, if we pin our hopes of eternal survival to love, if we glue our spirits to love, we too shall still be alive and eternally young, like love itself. For love is the very stuff of God. That is why it lasts forever (1 Cor 13:8). When death destroys the destructible, the indestructible remains. That is the point of Hebrews 12:26–28. In this passage, "what is shaken" refers to the entire created universe, and the "kingdom that cannot be shaken" refers to the love of God:

> His voice then shook the earth; but now he has promised, 'Yet once more I will shake not only the earth but also the heaven.' This phrase, 'Yet once more', indicates the removal of what is shaken, as of what has been made, in order that what cannot be shaken may remain. Therefore let us be grateful for receiving a kingdom that cannot be shaken, and thus let us offer to God acceptable worship, with reverence and awe; for our God is a consuming fire.

The fire is love. Love, like fire, destroys all its enemies, including "the last enemy" (1 Cor 15:26), death.

At the point of death, a great battle is waged for the heavyweight championship of the universe: in this corner Death, and in that corner Love. But death cannot change love; love changes death. Love changes the meaning of death, but death does not change the meaning of love. When fire and water meet, one must die. "Love is strong as death" (Song 8:6) because "many waters cannot quench love, neither can floods drown it" (Song 8:7). Death threatens love with extinction: "Love, thou shalt die." But love replies, in triumph, in the concluding words of Donne's great poem "Death, Be Not Proud": "Death, thou shalt die."

The end of the story of all Creation, all time and history, is prophesied here, as it is at the end of Revelation. Here is how God's love story ends: with endless life and love and heavenly marriage:

> Then I saw a new heaven and a new earth; for the first heaven and the first earth had passed away, and the sea [symbolic of death] was no more. And I saw the holy city, new Jerusalem,

coming down out of heaven from God, prepared as a bride adorned for her husband. And I heard a loud voice from the throne saying, "Behold, the dwelling of God is with men. He will dwell with them, and they shall be his people, and God himself will be with them; he will wipe away every tear from their eyes, and death shall be no more, neither shall there be mourning nor crying nor pain any more, for the former things have passed away." And he who sat upon the throne said, "Behold I make all things new." Also, he said, "Write this, for these words are trustworthy and true." And he said to me, "It is done! I am the Alpha and the Omega, the beginning and the end. To the thirsty I will give water without price from the fountain of the water of life" (Rev 21:1–6).

Did you hear that? Without payment! Our only qualification is thirst. The incredible offer is repeated again in Revelation 22:17:

The Spirit and the Bride [the Church] say, "Come." And let him who hears say, "Come." And let him who is thirsty come, let him who desires take the water of life without price.

Eternal joy, marriage to God, is "without price" because Love has already paid the price, on Calvary.

Love, you see, can do *anything*. Love alone can fill Ecclesiastes' emptiness—and yours. Love alone can satisfy Job's quest— and yours.